Flip Chart Games for Trainers

Flip Chart Games for Trainers

Graham Roberts-Phelps

Gower

© Graham Roberts-Phelps 1998

The materials that appear in this book, other than those quoted from prior sources, may be reproduced for education/training activities. There is no requirement to obtain special permission for such uses.

This permission statement is limited to reproduction of materials for educational or training events. Systematic or large-scale reproduction or distribution - or inclusion of items in publication for sale - may be carried out only with prior written permission from the publisher.

This edition published by
Gower Publishing Limited
Gower House
Croft Road
Aldershot
Hampshire GU11 3HR
England

Gower
Old Post Road
Brookfield
Vermont 05036
USA

Graham Roberts-Phelps has asserted his right under the Copyright, Designs and Patents Act 1988 to be identified as the author of this work.

British Library Cataloguing in Publication Data
Roberts-Phelps, Graham
   Flip chart games for trainers
   1. Management games 2. Employees - Training of
   I. Title
   658.3'12404

ISBN 0 566 08025 7

Library of Congress Cataloguing-in-Publication Data
Roberts-Phelps, Graham.
   Flip chart games for trainers / Graham Roberts-Phelps.
     p.   cm.
   Includes index.
   ISBN 0-566-08025-7
   1. Business presentations--Graphic methods. 2. Charts, diagrams.
 etc. 3. Teaching--Aids and devices. 4. Group games. I. Title.
HF5718.22.R65   1998
658.4'5--dc21   97-32769
                                                                                CIP

Typeset in Footlight by 80/20 Training Ltd and printed in Great Britain by the University Press, Cambridge.

Contents

Overview	1
50 Ideas to Improve your Use of the Flip Chart	3
Drawing Tips	7
Examples of Combining Shapes for Graphical Impact	9
Activities Cross-Reference	11

THE FLIP CHART ACTIVITIES 13

Action Plan	15
Anagram Quiz	18
Attitude Survey	21
Billboard	25
Brainstorm	28
Café Society	31
Cartoon Time	34
Change Planner	37
Criteria Grid	40
Competence Chart	43
Customer Charter	46
Do's and Don'ts	49
Driving Forces	51
F.A.Q.'s	54
Flowcharting	57
Goal Setting	60
Hopes and Concerns	63
How To's	66
Iceberg Chart	68
If I Were …	71
I Wish I Had	74
Jargon Jumble	77
Jigsaw Summary	80
Keyword Summary	83
Keys to Success	86

METAPHORS	89
MIND MAP	92
MNEMONIC CHALLENGE	95
MY SECRET	98
MY FAVOURITE	100
NEXT STEPS	102
NICKNAMES	104
OLD HABITS TO NEW	106
PARKING LOT	109
PICTOGRAM	112
PRIORITY MATRIX	115
PROBLEM-SOLVING GRAFFITI	118
PUZZLE PHRASES (REBUSES)	121
QUICK QUIZ	124
REASONS TO LEARN	127
SAY IT ANOTHER WAY	129
SEVEN QUESTION SUMMARY	132
SIX POINT PROFILE	134
STEP BY STEP	137
SWOT CHART	140
TEAM TALENTS	143
TEAM SOLUTIONS	145
TAKING SIDES	147
TOP TEN IDEAS	149
TRAINING STANDARDS	151
APPENDIX	**155**
QUOTATIONS	157
REBUSES	163
SOLUTIONS TO PUZZLE PHRASES	172

Overview

Flip Chart Games for Trainers is a collection of energising, ice-breaking, thought-provoking, creativity-boosting ideas using only a flip chart.

Each exercise is designed to make your training course more effective, interactive and involving.

Designed and collated by Graham Roberts-Phelps, each idea has been carefully tried and tested in a number of different training environments, including

- Management skills
- Customer service
- IT/PC Training
- Language training
- Sales skills
- Quality
- Teamwork
- Safety
- … and many others

If you have any suggestions for inclusion in a future volume, or have any questions regarding these activities please contact 80/20 Training Ltd on (44) 01908 587462.

50 Ideas to Improve your Use of the Flip Chart

1. Display where everybody can see it easily!

2. Use several flip charts for flexibility and ease of use.

3. Choose paper that is ruled or squared for more accurate drawing and neater writing.

4. Use chisel tip pens for width of line and clarity, also to create italic effects.

5. Move chart regularly to maintain interest.

6. Pin pages around the training room, this serves to visually reinforce learning points during the course.

7. Draw simple graphs and charts to represent numbers visually.

8. Keep eye contact with the group when reading or reviewing from the flip chart.

9. Carry a good set (10+) of flip chart pens with you at all times, making sure there are plenty of different colours.

10. Draw a coloured frame around the edge of a page.

11. Use different colours for bullets from the text.

12. Use different coloured headings and annotations.

13. Alternate colours - one line of red, one line blue.

14. Use primary colours for main headings and key points.

15. Use pastel or shades for effects - shadow, underline - and figures.

16. Even if you can't draw, illustrate your pages with shapes such as circles, boxes, etc.

17. Use dropped or large leading capitals for effect.

18. Vary the use of lower case, small capitals and large capitals.

19. Keep flip chart pages and have them typed up after the course for review and follow-up.

20. Use stencils for a neater appearance; perhaps make your own.

21. Prepare as much as possible beforehand.

22. Integrate your flip chart with the OHP slides.

23. Keep track of the bulk of pages you are turning over.

24. Get delegates to make contributions via the flip chart.

25. Always make sure spare pads will be available for your use.

26. Invest in some of the new coloured flip pads or the multicoloured flip pads.

27. Even at the end of the day try to keep your writing neat and not a scrawl.

28. Flip chart notes are invaluable for future sessions - don't forget to take them back to the office with you.

29. Make sure you have maximum visibility and clarity.

30. Your flip chart notes help the latecomer or absentee to 'catch up' with things.

31. Use your chart to provide participants with pride in accomplishment. Reward relative to their contribution.

32. Use your completed pages to create a sense of atmosphere-this is a training room not just a classroom.

33. Use your flip chart as a role model for all delegates-especially managers. Suggest that all managers will one day have a flip chart in their office.

34. Avoid writing close to the bottom of the page.

35. Consider using two or more flip charts. This will provide the opportunity to move around. It will also be a time saver, i.e. using previously prepared material on one and keeping the other for freshly generated ideas.

36. Make liberal use of the T-column.

37. Use a sheet as a visual reminder to respond to questions or issues that were deferred.

38. At the start of sessions, write a thought-provoking or humorous quotation on the flip chart as people enter the room. (Some examples are included in the appendix at the back of the manual.)

39. If your training room is set up in a U shape, keep the easel on the right as right-handers look to the right.

40. If possible, use water-based non-toxic markers that won't bleed through the paper onto other sheets.

41. Don't let a flip chart remain on the easel; it could serve as a distraction. Either flip it over, post on the wall or discard it.

42. Use a single colour of pen for each major topic, theme or unit. This facilitates the search for particular references.

43. Consider posting a flip chart on the wall labelled "unfinished business". Advise delegates to enter items on it at any time when it is apparent that some need is not being met.

44. On your "unfinished business" sheet you may consider using sub-categories to help delegates to better describe their needs.

45. If you are asking delegates to enter items on posted sheets you may consider taping a pen to the wall for convenient use.

46. At various times during the course, ask delegates to walk around the room to review the posted sheets.

47. Talk to the audience rather than to the flip chart. If, while entering data, you have a comment for the group, simply stop writing, turn completely around and make your statement.

48. Help build a humour-laden atmosphere via your flip chart. A few cartoons, funny quotations, poems which your delegates can check out before the start, at breaks and at lunch will garner a few chuckles from them and encourage interaction between participants.

49. Make notes lightly in pencil in advance and then ink over (pencil won't be seen by class).

50. Use masking tape to secure pages to wall, this is much better than pins or "Blu-Tack". If you use lengths of tape rolled with adhesive side outside-thereby becoming invisible - do remove if stacking pages for re-use.

Drawing Tips

With a bit of practice, you can easily learn to liven up your flip chart pages with a few hand drawn graphics.

Try them out first on normal size paper, perhaps tracing over printed cartoons or illustrations.

For a really accurate drawing, photocopy a printed drawing onto an OHP acetate slide and then project the image on to a flip chart. Carefully trace the image using marking pens.

A useful and interesting book on creating meaningful visual communication in business is **Atlas of Management Thinking** by Edward De Bono, 1981, published by Penguin.

Graphical Building Blocks

Circle	○	Oval	⬭
Square	▢	Triangle	△
Star	☆	Rectangle	▭

Faces and bodies

THINGS AND IDEAS

Idea

Team building

Time

Key skill or technique

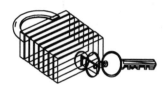

Money

Problem

Direction

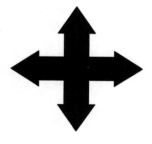

Examples of Combining Shapes for Graphical Impact

Activities Cross-Reference

Here is a summary of the activities and where they can be best used.

ICE-BREAKERS

My Secret
My Favourite
Nicknames
Attitude Survey
If I Were …
I Wish I Had
Competence Chart
Hopes and Concerns
Jargon Jumble
Puzzle Phrases (Rebuses)
Reasons to Learn

ENERGISERS

Old Habits To New
Priority Matrix
Problem-solving Graffiti
Anagram Quiz
If I Were …
Metaphors
Taking Sides
Jargon Jumble
Quick Quiz
Six Point Profile
Team Talents

DISCUSSION FORUMS

Step by Step
Parking Lot
SWOT Chart
Brainstorm
Customer Charter
Metaphors
Criteria Grid
Competence Chart
How To's
Reasons to Learn
F.A.Q.s

PROBLEM SOLVING

Priority Matrix
Say It Another Way
Team Solutions
Brainstorm
Change Planner
Criteria Grid
Driving Forces
Flowcharting
Iceberg Chart
Mind Map

SUMMARY ACTIVITIES

Action Plan
Billboard
Cartoon Time
Do's and Don'ts
Mnemonic Challenge
Next Steps
Goal Setting
Jigsaw Summary
Keyword Summary
Keys to Success
Seven Question Summary
Top Ten Ideas
Quick Quiz

THE FLIP CHART ACTIVITIES

Action Plan

APPLICATION

The purpose or outcome of any training course is probably the most important aspect of that training course. In ensuring that delegates achieve the maximum possible following a course, it is very important to allow time, either at key stages during or towards the end of the course, for them to gather their thoughts together and produce an action plan. This simple exercise allows a structured action plan to be developed based around key behaviours.

The four headings suggested here focus on behavioural aspects of any particular job. Such headings as Stop Doing, Start Doing, Do More Of and Do Less Of are very applicable to such things as telephone skills, customer service, assertiveness, time management, personal organisation, people management, etc. This activity is best used at the end of a training session or course. It may be used either in syndicates or individually.

PROCEDURE

- ☑ Draw the chart on a flip chart page.

- ☑ Using a flip chart page, ask delegates to prepare their own personal action plan, based on the course or training session, under each of the four headings.

- ☑ Allow 10 - 15 minutes. Supply flip chart paper and pens.

- ☑ Whilst delegates are working, circulate around the room and make sure that they are specifying their action points clearly enough. It is important that the action plans are practical and focused and really concentrate on things that the individual can do to implement improvements. For example, a delegate may write - *'To improve their telephone answering skills'*. This is really not specific enough, it would be better to say, *'Answer calls quicker, sound more friendly when answering the telephone, and keep customers on hold for the minimum length of time'*.

- ☑ Display pages around the room and ask delegates to present their plan to the rest of the main group.

Action Plan

Start Doing	Stop Doing

Do More Of	**Do Less Of**
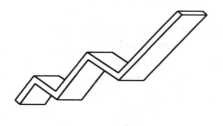	

FLIP 1

RELATED FLIP CHARTS

Top Ten Ideas, How To's, Next Steps, Old Habits to New.

VARIATIONS AND NOTES

- ☑ If you wish to, in a larger group or course, delegates can work together in threes, fours, or larger groups to summarise the key action points for each of the groups.

- ☑ These action points can be kept, typed up or reviewed later in a review session or workshop following the training course to discuss how they have progressed in implementing their actions.

- ☑ This type of Action Plan can also serve as a good tool for managers and training sponsors to follow up the training and the effectiveness of the course.

- ☑ Have the delegates take their flip chart page away with them so as to put it in their work area to review and keep to hand as they implement the ideas.

Anagram Quiz

APPLICATION

This exercise is useful where the learning takes the form of memorising information. For example, learning technical terms, product names or features, branch locations, computer jargon, or any other pieces of information which need to be remembered. In the example are the three anagrams of the words PUZZLE, CLEVER and TRICKY respectively. This can be used where fact needs to be remembered and retained for, say, an examination. An interesting and unusual quiz exercise to test retention and understanding.

PREPARATIONS

1) Prepare ten questions and answers based on the training course or session; these should have one or two word answers.

2) Jumble the letters (or numbers!) from each answer and write on the flip chart in a random order and position.

PROCEDURE

- ☑ Ask delegates to copy anagrams from the flip chart, exactly as they are written.

- ☑ Allow 5-10 minutes.

- ☑ Read out your first question, ask delegates to pick an answer and write (1) (for question) next to it.

- ☑ Continue with all ten questions.

- ☑ If you wish, you may ask the delegates to explain the one or two word answer further to check they have understood the lesson.

RELATED FLIP CHARTS

Jargon Jumble, Keyword Summary, Jigsaw Summary, Pictogram and Quick Quiz.

Anagram Quiz

▶ Unjumble the words to find the answer to the questions

LEPZUZ

RELVEC

KRICTY

FLIP 2

VARIATIONS AND NOTES

- ☑ There is no limit to the way this exercise can be run. For example, you can ask delegates to work in pairs or groups and detect the words and then write definitions of the meanings.

- ☑ Another variation would be to divide the group into two or a series of groups and have them select ten key words or phrases, produce the anagrams and then swap papers for the other team to guess which words they relate to or represent.

Attitude Survey

APPLICATION

Attitude is one of the critical aspects of many jobs today; not only in such fields as customer service, sales and team work, but also in the roles of manager, consultant, professional nurse, teacher and so on. Many people find it difficult to either discuss attitude openly or indeed measure exactly what is meant by a positive attitude and a negative attitude. We all know when we experience somebody with a negative attitude, but exactly how do we know? What is it they do that prompts us to realise such thoughts?

As well as discussing attitude in general, this exercise also has a great deal of benefit when focused on a particular topic or issue. For example, what attitudes may people have towards such things as implementing a new policy, moving office, the appointment of a new manager, a new organisational structure, taking over or merging with another company, changes through redundancy, re-deployment or skill retraining, implementing new technology, changes in working patterns or shifts, and general uncertainties about their job or role? It is often very beneficial to bring these types of attitudes out in the open where they can be expressed and discussed and where necessary adjustments or clarification can be made. It is important to create an atmosphere of openness and approach this exercise non-judgementally.

Perhaps highlight that there is no such thing as a good or a bad attitude, just simply a certain way of looking at things. For example, two people may look at a glass of water and one describe it as half full and the other describe it as half empty. Both are, of course, correct. In general - as one observer noted - we need a world full of optimistic sales people and pessimistic security guards!

This is an application for any topic where there may be mixed feelings, ideas, attitudes or learning resistance. It allows trainers to discuss these issues openly.

Attitude Survey

▶ Identify examples of good and bad attitudes

+ Ve  - Ve

FLIP 3

PROCEDURE

- ☑ Write "Attitudes" on the top of a flip page with a "+" and a "—" on the left and right hand side respectively.

- ☑ Ask delegates to work in small groups and list their attitudes towards a given idea, plan, topic, issue, etc. Provide flip chart paper and pens. (Attitudes are often expressed as beliefs, values, generalisations, opinions, judgements and so on.)

- ☑ Place each attitude on either the "+" (positive) or "-" (negative) part of the page (neutral should be central).

- ☑ Allow 10 - 15 minutes.

- ☑ Review and discuss in teams or main group.

RELATED FLIP CHARTS

Hopes and Concerns, Change Planner, Iceberg Chart.

VARIATIONS AND NOTES

- ☑ This exercise can also be done individually with people working independently on their own thoughts towards something. The thinking in working in groups is that people are often able to support each other in identifying these key attitudes, something of which they may not be conscious.

- ☑ Following the exercise, time could be taken to discover issues such as how do you turn a negative into a positive attitude, and what are some of the factors that contribute to either supporting a positive attitude or creating more of a negative attitude. Discuss whether these factors are external i.e. things outside of ourselves or internal i.e. in our own thought patterns. It is perhaps interesting to note that one event that may motivate somebody else and encourage them to try harder can also demotivate and generate a negative attitude or expectation in others.

- ☑ Discuss how our own expectations often lead to a positive or negative attitude: how if you expect something to turn out well, often you may have a positive attitude, whereas if you expect the worst to happen then this may lead you to a negative attitude.

☑ Ask delegates to re-form into their groups and discuss attitude in respect of the attitudes that they have to confront or deal with in their work. For example, if they are managers or supervisors they must know how to deal with people with a negative attitude or with a very positive, and perhaps unrealistic, attitude. This is also true of customer service, sales, technical, professional, teaching, nursing and other staff. Ask them to discuss whether it is possible to change somebody else's attitude, and if so how this is done. Perhaps ask them to start by considering any examples of whether they have been able to change somebody's thinking from either negative or positive or indeed from positive to negative, because of the things they have done or said or events that they have created. For example, a customer may have had a very unhappy and negative attitude about a particular organisation, which was changed because of the care, concern and empathy demonstrated by other staff in relation to a complaint. Just this small amount of time spent can actually turn around a customer's attitude quite dramatically.

Billboard

APPLICATION

This is an unusual way of summarising course content.

We are all of us bombarded by billboards, advertising posters, slogans, shop signs, even fly-posters every single day. The billboard or the advertiser's goal is to make sure that they give their products or points prominence: to make sure we see it, that our eyes are attracted to it and, most of all, that we remember it.

This exercise asks delegates to design such a billboard or poster, one that they may like to display around the training room, their workplace or indeed anywhere.

It is light-hearted fun, interactive and most of all a pertinent way of summarising the key learning points from any training session no matter what duration or type. It can be used for almost any topic of training from management skills to customer service, sales to science, technical expertise to teaching.

It is a particularly useful exercise to use when any major point or key theme has been introduced and needs to be reinforced. For example, a new approach to customer service, a new way of teamworking and quality initiative.

PROCEDURE

- ☑ Direct delegates to work in pairs or small groups.
- ☑ Give each pair a sheet of flip paper, and coloured pens.
- ☑ Display around the room.

Billboard

▶ Design an advertising hoarding or poster to "sell" the main points from today's course

▶ First generate as MANY ideas as possible

▶ Then, evaluate and select the best few

BUY THIS!

FLIP 4

- ☑ Explain to delegates that they are going to design an advertising poster or billboard to display in the training room to summarise the key points from today. Explain that it should ideally be memorable, visual, eye-catching and most of all, enable people to remember the most important aspects and want to remember and implement the ideas. Ask them to think about some of the billboards or posters that they see either around them day to day or on the way to work. They probably will be unable to remember that many, but we see them all and they all make an impression on us.

- ☑ Ask group to vote for best posters.

- ☑ Explain that it is important that they first take time to generate as many ideas as possible, no matter how crazy daft or outlandish these may first appear. This is the approach that many advertising agencies will take; they will have a creative period where they go through a whole series of different ideas brainstorming anything they can think of as a theme. These are then sifted through, sorted, evaluated and a shortlist produced. One of these will then be developed as a finished poster.

- ☑ Delegates should take about 10 - 15 minutes to brainstorm the ideas then a further 10 - 15 minutes to evaluate and design their finished poster.

RELATED FLIP CHARTS

Jigsaw Summary, Keyword Summary, Next Steps, Pictogram, Do's and Don'ts.

VARIATIONS AND NOTES

- ☑ Perhaps award a prize to the team or group with the best idea, the best visuals or the most novel approach.

- ☑ Once you have reviewed the final posters for each group ask them to review some of their more way-out ideas. This is often very amusing, although frequently people are far more conservative in their thinking than you might first expect.

- ☑ Ask delegates to vote for the poster that they like the best.

- ☑ Following the training course find somebody with a bent for graphic design and see if you can have them produce the poster on a computer for displaying around the offices/workplace.

- ☑ If you are running a series of courses over a period of time on the same topic, then the posters can be collected and perhaps used as a post-course review at a later stage.

Brainstorm

APPLICATION

This is useful as both a training energiser and ice-breaker or a practical way of generating ideas and suggestions. How to improve standards or overcome specific problems or situations that may stand in the way of implementing improvements to working practices.

It has proved particularly suitable for supervisory or management level staff who may be involved in initiating, implementing or maintaining policy and procedures.

Brainstorming is a very well established and useful tool in developing new ideas, concepts and thought patterns, and can be used for virtually any topical subject. The key requirements are, an open environment where people can make ideas freely without fear of judgement, criticism or ridicule, enough time, enough people, enough flip chart paper and enough focus. The trigger question is usually critical in developing a good brainstorming session.

The question should highlight some shortfall, issue, problem or dilemma and ask how that could be improved by specific or pre-defined amounts. For example, how could we reduce customer complaints by 50% in the next three months? How can applications for registration be improved and take half the time they are now? How can we reduce costs by 10% across all departments? How can we reduce staff turnover? How can we improve staff punctuality? How can we improve customer service in ways the customer can measure and appreciate? How can we motivate people to do a better job?

PROCEDURE

- ☑ List instructions on the flip chart.

- ☑ Form delegates into groups of 4 - 7 and select facilitator.

Generate as many ideas as possible

FLIP 5

- ☑ Provide each group with flip chart paper and pens.
- ☑ Provide the brainstorming focus or trigger question.
- ☑ Offer a prize for the team with the most ideas -remember - *any idea is a good idea.*
- ☑ Allow 20 - 30 minutes.
- ☑ Review each group in turn.

    (optional: ask each group to select "best three ideas".)

RELATED FLIP CHARTS

Change Planner, Driving Forces, Iceberg Charts, Team Solutions, Top Ten Ideas.

VARIATIONS AND NOTES

- ☑ Perhaps run a warm-up brainstorming session for just ten minutes to give delegates the opportunity to practise this way of thinking. A good example would be to ask them to list as many applications they can think of for a common plastic credit card other than buying things. A group of 3 - 6 people given 10 - 15 minutes should be able to generate at least 30 ideas, many of which are probably far more common than you might imagine. (Try this exercise and you will discover what I mean!) Perhaps introduce this exercise by running a lateral thinking puzzle.

Café Society

APPLICATION

A good discussion exercise that breaks the normal "talk and talk" approach to training.

This can make a refreshing and original alternative to the traditional format of a workshop or training course. It does require a degree of courage and concentration on the part of the trainer, as you are basically leaving the room open to delegates to roam as and where they choose from table to table and topic to topic.

Suitable applications where this has been used successfully are such things as a quality workshops, where each table may feature a different aspect of quality. Another application might be in management skills training, where rather than put managers and supervisors on a formal course, you could have them discuss the issues which are relevant to their work situation and learn from each other through discussion and sharing of ideas.

It can also be used very successfully in the learning of technical skills, such as computer expertise or understanding finance. For example, a series of computers set up in each corner of the room, each one with a champion or trainer running a different type of training session. They could be running mail merging, graphic design and so on.

PROCEDURE

- ☑ Prepare the room with four or more tables or circles of chairs, perhaps using the corners of the room.

- ☑ Write a different trigger question, topic or task on a flip chart page in each corner or area.

- ☑ Start by dividing delegates equally around the areas and appoint subject champions. They should facilitate the conversation, prevent arguments and record important points on the flip chart.

- ☑ Explain that they can move around the room, moving from area to area, in any sequence as often as they like - as their interest or curiosity takes them - with the exception, of course, of the subject champions.

Café Society

▶ Each corner of the room is a different discussion group

▶ Circulate around the room, as you feel, dropping in and out of conversation as the mood takes you

FLIP 6

- ☑ Allow 20 - 30 minutes and then review the outcome of the discussions from each corner.

RELATED FLIP CHARTS

SWOT Chart, Team Solutions, Parking Lot, Next Steps, Seven Question Summary.

VARIATIONS AND NOTES

- ☑ Use a timer to set a limit of say 20 minutes. At the end of 20 minutes sound a gong or hooter and ask everybody to change to the next table or move around one table to the left. This will allow a bigger group to stay structured whilst still having an informal and personal air about the workshop.

- ☑ Before the course discuss with delegates what topics they would like to discuss or focus on, these will give you the topics or subjects for each table or area.

- ☑ Each of the different subject areas or circles could also be used in a brainstorming exercise (see previous exercise). Delegates could simply circulate from table to table adding ideas to the topic being brainstormed in each section.

- ☑ At regular points during the session or during the day, pull delegates together as a main group and ask each subject champion to highlight or present the key issues, topics or observations that were discussed or revealed during their session.

Cartoon Time

APPLICATION

Good as a course energiser and to review key ideas in a humorous fashion.

Cartoons are very popular amongst almost everybody. Very few people escape childhood without regularly reading some form of comic or picture book, whether this was Marvel or Rupert, the Beano or Enid Blyton. Today most business journals, newspapers and magazines will regularly feature cartoons or cartoon strips.

As perhaps a session starter, share with a group some favourite examples of your own; be careful, of course, to observe any copyright wishes.

Discuss peoples favourite cartoon or cartoonist, for instance, Gary Larson, Dilbert, Giles and so on.

This exercise is best used with any training topic where a person's skill is involved. For example telephone skills, customer service, manual handling, managing people, greeting customers, selling, teamwork, motivation, teaching, presenting, meetings and so on.

PROCEDURE

- ☑ Draw as overleaf (or similar) onto flip chart.

- ☑ Ask delegates to work in pairs or threes.

- ☑ Explain that they should: design and draw a simple cartoon or humorous scene related to the training subject.

- ☑ Suggest that delegates approach this task by first discussing and sketching some sample ideas of what the cartoon may look like or what its content or punchline may be, then select the person in the group who perhaps has the best artistic hand, and put together a simple but effective cartoon. Discuss how faces, bodies, objects and so on can be used simply to create a cartoon effect (see Drawing Tips in the introduction of this book for more help, or refer to any of the excellent books available on such things as how to draw cartoons).

Cartoon Time

▶ Design and draw a simple cartoon or humorous scene about the subject being covered today

FLIP 7

- ☑ Allow 15 minutes.
- ☑ Post around room and review.
- ☑ Ask group to vote for the best or the funniest.

RELATED FLIP CHARTS

Jigsaw Summary, Metaphors, Mind Map, Pictogram, Step by Step.

VARIATIONS AND NOTES

- ☑ Prior to the training course, design, draw or find a cartoon that you can use and have delegates suggest a suitable punchline or text.

- ☑ Prior to the training course, find some old photographs or Victorian-type sketching of which delegates could then add their own bubbles and explanations relating to the course in question. For example, if your course is about meetings and time management then use an old fashioned picture of people discussing things around a table - maybe delegates can come up with some witty quotes to put for the key figures.

- ☑ As an alternative to using flip chart paper give delegates write-on film and some acetate pens to design directly on to a foil.

Change Planner

APPLICATION

A good activity for any session that addresses changing or altering the status quo.

Change today is commonplace in almost every organisation, big or small. Observers and psychologists have noted that the human condition resists change, almost irrationally. "Better the devil you know than the devil you don't know", is an attitude of mind that many people, indeed most of us, will experience from time to time. This activity asks delegates to focus on this change or one aspect of change, and work through it in a practical and positive manner.

The changing question could be one of many, ranging from imposed change due to re-organisation or personal change, for whatever reason.

For example, this exercise can be used when discussing actions arising from the training course, focusing on some aspect of impending change that delegates or attendees will have to face, such as the introduction of new technology, moving to a new job, taking on new responsibilities, and so on.

It can also be useful in helping people to come to terms with change, breaking them down into a series of chunks, therefore reducing the resistance to change.

PROCEDURE

☑ Draw the following table onto a flip chart page.

☑ Ask delegates to work in pairs or small groups and select changes arising from the course or session. Alternatively you may have pre-selected a change issue for discussion.

☑ Supply the flip chart paper and pens.

☑ Delegates should list points under headings in the boxes.

☑ Allow 15 - 20 minutes or as required.

Change Planner

▶ Consider something that you would like to change or improve

▶ Make notes in each of the four boxes to help you plan this

Key Milestones	Likely Obstacles
Benefits	Concerns

FLIP 8

☑ Ask each group to present its chart to the rest of the participants.

RELATED FLIP CHARTS

Action Plan, Driving Forces, Hopes and Concerns, Attitude Survey.

VARIATIONS AND NOTES

☑ You may want to vary the headings in each of the four boxes depending on the type of change, for example, when implementing a personal change generated by individuals the headings might read Key Milestones, Likely Obstacles, What's Stopping Me, What Can Help Me.

☑ Following on from this exercise, you could ask delegates to return to their pairs or small groups and take one or more of the likely obstacles and develop a series of ideas or actions that could help prevent or overcome these barriers.

☑ If delegates have listed more concerns than benefits or more obstacles than milestones, once again it might be worth re-directing them, either through general discussion or by forming them back into groups to achieve more of a balance.

☑ Discuss as a group summary how we resist change, often unconsciously coming up with reasons and excuses why not to change, even though we know it might be good for us and we know that once we have a new perspective we will gain new benefits.

☑ Highlight examples of your own where you have perhaps changed or developed and how this has helped you. Discuss such things as moving house, changing careers, moving jobs and so on.

Criteria Grid

APPLICATION

A good exercise for deciding or examining more complex issues such as quality processes, standards, product design, job specification or anything that involves balancing several important variables.

This exercise is particularly suited for complex issues where an analytical or detailed approach is required. For example, the benchmark between quality and customer service standards, deciding on priorities and job responsibilities, allocating work and project tasks, allocating and deciding on budget priorities.

It is important that enough time is spent not only in running this exercise, but also discussing the outcomes and differences of opinion that may arise.

It requires delegates to consider these things not only carefully but also in relation to each other.

PROCEDURE

- ☑ Draw the grid on flip chart.

- ☑ Define variables for the elements A - E that you are comparing, e.g. factors in choosing a venue for a conference (or more as needed).

- ☑ Try to limit the elements to five or six key issues. Remember the more elements you have the more complex the model may become and the more issues will have to be discussed.

- ☑ Form trainees into groups.

- ☑ Provide flip chart paper and pens.

- ☑ Direct them to assess each element against each other and mark the most important in the box: e.g. "Which is more important, A or B?" In the venue example; "Is good parking (A) more or less important that leisure facilities(B)?" Write the letter of the MOST important factor in the box. Total scores for each element. Review and discuss.

Criteria Grid

▶ Decide the relative importance of each criterion, i.e. is A more important than B?... etc.

	A	B	C	D	E
A	X				
B		X			
C			X		
D				X	
E					X

FLIP 9

RELATED FLIP CHARTS

Priority Matrix, Iceberg Chart, Goal Setting, Flowcharting, Driving Forces, Change Planner.

VARIATIONS AND NOTES

- ☑ Instead of you choosing the elements and deciding what the critical factors are, run a pre-exercise activity and have delegates decide the top six or seven key elements involved in the application they are considering. For example, if you were discussing a hotel or conference venue, rather than giving delegates what you consider to be the critical aspects, have them make this decision.

- ☑ Have each group present their conclusions to the rest of the group and invite comment and discussion. Display all the completed pages around the room and highlight any discrepancy or trends that may exist. Re-form delegates back into groups and ask them to re-consider or change any of their ratings following the main group discussion and to arrive at a definitive model.

- ☑ Discuss how they changed their thoughts and attitudes through group discussion, if at all.

Competence Chart

APPLICATION

A valuable exercise to clearly define competence levels for any job, individual position or process. It can be used in a variety of subject areas e.g. interviewing/recruitment, coaching, safety, quality, management, etc.

PROCEDURE

- ☑ Draw the table overleaf on a flip chart page. Ask delegates to copy the table.

- ☑ Initiate a short discussion to agree what is meant by the work 'Competence' and ask the group to volunteer a piece of knowledge, skill, attitude and an example of behaviour to see whether they have understood.

- ☑ Form into small groups or pairs.

- ☑ Provide flip chart paper and pens.

- ☑ Ask delegates to specify a job task, process etc that is relevant to the training course and ask delegates to identify: key knowledge elements, skills and techniques, activities and day to day behaviours that combine together to represent 'competence'. They should write their notes on flip chart pages.

- ☑ Allow 10 - 15 minutes.

- ☑ Display around the room and discuss.

RELATED FLIP CHARTS

How To's, Attitude Survey, Keys to Success, Old Habits to New, Team Talents.

Competence Matrix

▶ Identify key SKILLS, ATTITUDES, BEHAVIOURS and KNOWLEDGE that are needed to be considered "competent" for the training topic

Knowledge	Skills
Attitudes	Behaviours

FLIP 10

VARIATIONS AND NOTES

- ☑ Once all the groups have presented their competence matrix pages, ask them to make a note of any additional ideas other groups have suggested for each of the four headings, Knowledge, Skills, Attitudes and Behaviours. Then ask the group to re-form and prioritise the elements in each box. For example, they may have a list of different skills needed in that role, ask them to discuss and list them in order of priority - which is the most important etc. Allow 10 - 15 minutes and re-form the group to again display their different lists, this time using a new piece of flip chart paper.

- ☑ Re-form the groups and ask them to discuss each of the different highlighted items with either a plus or a minus as to whether they think its something they do well or not very well and could improve.

- ☑ Following this exercise re-form groups into small groups or pairs and ask them to discuss if they think there is any link between Knowledge, Skills, Attitudes and Behaviour.

Customer Charter

APPLICATION

For use in any customer service or quality session (NB: "customer" can of course be an internal customer as well as external).

As a way of introducing this exercise, perhaps collect some customer charters from your own or related businesses. Many hotels, restaurants, banks and public utilities have leaflets defining their customer standards. Read these out and review them as a way of introducing this exercise.

This exercise can be used not only in customer service or quality sessions, but also to define standards of teamwork, communication, meeting guidelines, purchasing procedures and the internal standards or functions of a particular support department or team.

PROCEDURE

- ☑ Draw the template on a flip chart.
- ☑ Form trainees into small groups (4 - 6 people).
- ☑ It is worth modelling this text - get in an example of the rights, standards charters etc and make sure everyone has understood.
- ☑ Supply the flip chart paper and pens.
- ☑ Ask them to write a "customer charter" defining the rights, standards and minimum expectations for a given group of "customers".
- ☑ Allow 15 - 20 minutes or as required.
- ☑ Post around room and ask each group to present.
- ☑ Discuss issues and ideas

RELATED FLIP CHARTS

Competence Chart, Criteria Grid, Café Society, Brainstorm, Mind Map.

Customer Charter

▶ Write a "Customer Charter", defining the rights and standards your "customers" can expect.

FLIP 11

VARIATIONS AND NOTES

☑ Prior to the training or following this exercise, ask the "customers" who are being focused on in this session to compile their own "customer charter" of what they would like to have as standards and expectations. If done before running this exercise, this can be revealed after the delegates have arrived at their own customer charter to see if they do, in fact, match and have the same issues and standards. For example, an internal personnel department might have a certain set of criteria they believe they can offer to other managers and staff within an organisation, which may be different to the expectation and standards that the staff and managers perceive the personnel department as providing for them.

☑ Following the group discussion, ask delegates to re-form into their groups and edit and review their customer charter based on the points made during the group discussion and any observations that may have come from their "customers".

☑ Encourage delegates to word each element or statement in a way that is clear, focused and precise in its definition.

☑ Following the group review session, run a short exercise asking delegates to discuss how the customer charter may be implemented, or how the standards can be guaranteed, or indeed what recourse customers may have if the standards are not achieved. This will also make sure that the standards specified are measurable.

☑ An alternative discussion may be structured around how you can avoid this customer charter becoming not just pleasant platitudes and well-meaning intentions, but turn it into a real and practical way of delivering customer satisfaction.

Do's and Don'ts

APPLICATION

A quick, easy and highly effective way of capturing key ideas, techniques, skills, behaviours or work practices in a training session. One of the key trends over the last few years has been to benchmark or model standards, or best practice in many areas. This very practical activity allows delegates to define best practice for any number of different skill areas or practices. Typical applications might include telephone skills, time management, managing meetings, communication skills, business writing, team building, and so on.

PROCEDURE

- ☑ Draw the columns on the flip chart. Label one column DO and one column DON'T.
- ☑ Form delegates into pairs or small groups.
- ☑ Supply the flip chart paper and pens.
- ☑ Allow 10 - 15 minutes or as required.
- ☑ Ask them to list a given number (5 - 10, etc) of do's and don'ts on a given topic or skill.
- ☑ Post around the room; ask each group to review in turn.

RELATED FLIP CHARTS

Criteria Grid, Competence Chart.

VARIATIONS AND NOTES

- ☑ You could give different groups a variety of topics to work on in the same training course. If running a training session on safety, ask one group to focus on lifting, one on VDU safety, one on fire safety.
- ☑ Run a short discussion on how people often know what they should or shouldn't be doing but do the opposite in daily work or routine activities.

Do's and Don'ts

▶ List ten Do's and ten Don'ts that represent "best practice"

DO	DON'T

FLIP 12

Driving Forces

APPLICATION

Useful for identifying issues regarding change implementation, problem solving, goal setting or making improvements.

It is a well documented fact that in any change situation there are two sets of forces at work. The driving force is striving for improvement or change and the restraining force is standing against that change or in some way holding back the progress. This exercise allows delegates to gain a better understanding of what these forces are, create labels and identify them and begin the process of maximising the driving forces and minimising or overcoming some of the restraining forces where needed.

This exercise can be used in a wide range of different applications, and is ideal for any quality customer service or management change initiative.

PROCEDURE

- ☑ Draw the chart on a flip chart page.

- ☑ Form trainees into small groups.

- ☑ Lead a short discussion or presentation on how any change or progress situation has two sets of forces. Highlight that these forces can either be external to either ourselves or the organisation or internal, things of our own creation or making. Explain that this exercise will allow you to identify what these are and begin to understand how they can be maximised or overcome.

- ☑ Ask delegates to summarise the forces at work in a given situation as either driving forces (moving forward) or restraints (holding back)

- ☑ Supply flip chart paper and pens.

- ☑ Allow 15 - 20 minutes.

Forces Field Analysis

▶ Identify the Driving Forces and Restraints

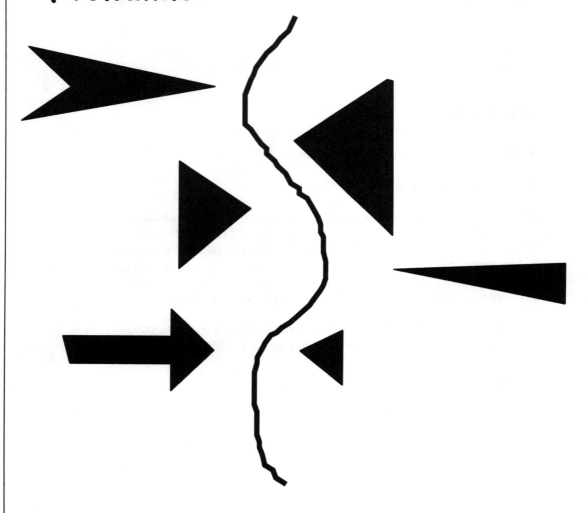

FLIP 13

- ☑ Post pages around room and ask each group to review.
- ☑ Run discussion on how best to remove or reduce restraining forces.

RELATED FLIP CHARTS

Attitude Survey, Hopes and Concerns, Flowcharting, Old Habits to New, Reasons to learn, SWOT Chart.

VARIATIONS AND NOTES

- ☑ Add an option about prioritising these forces in terms of likely effect and the ease or difficulty of changing them.
- ☑ Re-form delegates into their groups and ask them to discuss ways of how to maximise one or more driving force and how to overcome the different restraining forces. Are they real or imagined?
- ☑ Form delegates into groups and ask them to consider what they can do as managers now that they have identified these different forces.

F.A.Q.'s

APPLICATION

A good way of increasing interaction and identifying key issues and objectives, it also allows delegates to share their existing knowledge and experience. (NB: F.A.Q. = Frequently Asked Question, and is a term popularised by the Internet). The questions might be about the course or training topic or other frequent questions trainees are asked and have to answer.

This exercise is particularly suited to any situation where people are having to provide information as part of their job. For example, customer service, telephone staff, technical engineers, help desk staff, teachers, professionals, doctors, receptionists, supervisors and so on. It is based on the premise that some questions occur again and again, whereas some questions do not. By better preparing for the frequently asked questions in advance they can definitely improve and maximise their performance and assistance level.

PROCEDURE

- ☑ Draw the following on a flip chart.
- ☑ Form trainees into small groups or pairs.
- ☑ Ask them to list some F.A.Q.'s - either about the topic or that they have to answer as part of their job.
- ☑ Before setting the delegates the task, discuss some of the questions that they may get regularly so that they are clear about the task in hand. Stress the importance of using the questions that are asked frequently.
- ☑ Supply flip chart paper and pens.
- ☑ Allow 10 minutes, then swap pages between groups.
- ☑ Ask group to generate answers for as many questions as possible.

F.A.Q.'s

▶ List 5 or more Frequently Asked Questions (F.A.Q.'s) that you either have or have to answer as part of your job

▶ Swap pages and generate answers

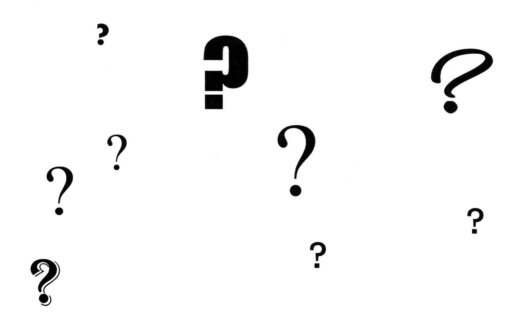

FLIP 14

RELATED FLIP CHARTS

Flowcharting, Jargon Jumble, Keyword Summary, Anagram Quiz, Problem Solving, Graffiti

VARIATIONS AND NOTES

- ☑ Re-form delegates into groups and ask them to work through each of their answers in turn, further polishing their wording and sentence structure to achieve clarity of response.

- ☑ You may choose to continue this exercise by role playing some of the different questions and testing the answers at which the delegates have arrived. Are they deliverable in a normal everyday conversational style? Can they be improved through practice?

- ☑ Discuss practical ways that these points can be remembered and applied. Is it practical to use scripts or prompt cards? Do these need to be memorised? Is simply working through them in this manner on this exercise help enough to enable you to be ready and prepared for regularly asked questions?

Flowcharting

APPLICATION

To summarise and check understanding of key or new processes, procedures or operations.

Flowcharting is a useful and valued visual way of organising processes, thoughts and frequencies in any activity. It can be used in a variety of different situations and subjects, for example, in operating procedures, security checks, time management, customer service, problem solving, serving customers, organisational issues and many others.

You might choose to start the session by drawing some of the different flowcharting symbols on the flip chart and explaining their definition. Whilst rarely used outside technical scientific or computer fields, some of these symbols can be successfully and usefully adapted for this exercise.

PROCEDURE

- ☑ Prepare a flip chart page as follows overleaf.

- ☑ Direct delegates - working in pairs or small groups - to prepare a flowchart of a process, procedure or operation related to the training topic.

- ☑ Supply the flip chart paper and pens.

- ☑ Illustrate by means of a simple example, for instance - making a hot drink.

- ☑ Allow 15 - 20 minutes or as needed.

- ☑ Post pages around the room and ask groups to present and review.

Flowcharting

▶ Summarise the key steps or ideas generated today as a flowchart

(Here are some symbols you might use)

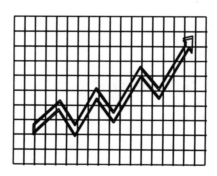

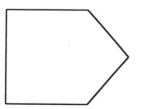

FLIP 15

RELATED FLIP CHARTS

Do's and Don'ts, Step by Step.

VARIATIONS AND NOTES

- ☑ If you have one large process you can choose to break down the process into different sections, giving one to each pair or small group on which to focus. For example, in processing an insurance claim form there may be several steps. Ask each group to identify the flow of information, paperwork and customer contact for each section.

- ☑ From this exercise re-form the groups again and ask them to review their flow chart and come up with a new model, overcoming any unnecessary steps, simplifying procedures and speeding up certain tasks by running things in parallel.

- ☑ It would be useful to discuss how this sequence or procedure came into being. Did it simply evolve over time or did in fact somebody sit down and design the optimum plan? (Most sequences or processes are a combination of the two.)

Goal Setting

APPLICATION

Goal setting is at the heart of both many personal and business performance programmes. Setting clear and specific objectives is essential for effective teamwork and management control.

This short activity can be used either as a tool for setting personal or business goals or as an end of course action plan.

It serves as a useful reminder of how to set goals and the benefit in doing so.

Typical applications might include: to set personal improvement goals following a course, identify the next steps, identify problems and issues that need to be resolved by setting them as goals, creating measures for assessing performance and improvement.

It is suitable for use in almost any training course.

PROCEDURE

- ☑ Transfer the suggested (overleaf), or a similar table, to a flip chart page. Set the scene by some reference to the importance of setting goals and objectives in harnessing our attention and energy.

- ☑ Set the scope of goal setting focus i.e. business/personal, long/short, big/small, etc; or simply ask delegates to consider their goals and actions arising from the training.

- ☑ Ask each person to prepare an example page.

- ☑ Allow 10 - 15 minutes.

- ☑ Each person to present individually.

Goal Setting

▶ Select a challenging and realistic goal and make some notes in each of the boxes below

What?	Why?
When?	How?

FLIP 16

RELATED FLIP CHARTS

Old Habits to New, Change Planner, Top Ten Ideas

VARIATIONS AND NOTES

- ☑ After delegates have set their own goals, ask them to work in small groups and list the most common points from their group.

- ☑ Re-form delegates into a large group and ask them to select one goal and develop a detailed "Action Plan" for that goal or objective.

- ☑ Ask delegates to schedule or call a meeting with you to follow-up from the session and review their progress towards their goals.

- ☑ Ask delegates to use the SMART model to test their goals, that is, whether they are Specific, Measurable, Achievable, Realistic and Time-bounded.

Hopes and Concerns

APPLICATION

Delegates on a training course are usually there for a variety of reasons, at one end of the scale, keen and uninhibited in their enthusiasm, at the other, reserved and nervous about what the course may involve. This means delegates' expectations will vary considerably.

Therefore, this a useful activity for the beginning of a training course or session. It establishes objectives and confirms resistance or concerns towards the course and its content that delegates may feel.

It also allows delegates to express their reservations and concerns openly as well as airing some more positive expectations for the event.

It is particularly suitable for any course that involves new technology, re-organisation, personal change, or a steep learning curve, or that is being run where morale is low.

PROCEDURE

- ☑ Draw the suggested chart on to a flip chart page.

- ☑ Explain that this exercise will allow delegates to express their reservations and concerns openly as well as some more positive expectations for the event.

- ☑ Organise delegates in pairs or small groups.

- ☑ Ask delegates to work amongst themselves, first discussing and listing their hopes for the course, followed by any concerns or reservations, course content or issues connected with it.

- ☑ Allow 10 - 15 minutes.

- ☑ When the time is up, post flip pages around the room. Discuss issues and summarise key themes arising.

RELATED FLIP CHARTS

Reasons to Learn, Mind Map.

Hopes and Concerns

▶ **Discuss and identify your hopes for the course and any concerns you might have – list them here**

Hopes	Concerns

FLIP 17

VARIATIONS AND NOTES

- ☑ Refer back to the delegates' hopes and concerns and connect the different sessions and modules from the course that address these specifically.

- ☑ At the end of the course, ask delegates to review their Hopes and Concerns pages and discuss if their hopes have been realised and whether concerns have be addressed in whole or in part.

- ☑ Instead of working in groups, run one large group session, facilitating input around a central flip chart.

How To's

APPLICATION

Increasingly, training is being required to provide practical solutions to day to day problems. Whilst learning is a benefit in its own right, it is important that skills and knowledge result in pragmatic solutions to delegate's specific learning objectives and situations.

This technique can also be used to test comprehension and knowledge retention at the end of the course or session.

It can be used on a variety of different courses, including computer training, mechanical or technical training, people skills, etc.

PROCEDURE

- Before running this exercise, prepare in advance a number of "How to's …" questions and list on a flip chart page. This should relate to course learning points.

- Form delegates into pairs or small groups.

- Ask delegates to consider one or more question(s) (as time allows) and prepare a short presentation that answers each point.

- Allow 15 - 20 minutes.

- Each group takes it in turn to present their answers.

RELATED FLIP CHARTS

Billboard, Jigsaw, Seven Question Summary, Top Ten Ideas

VARIATIONS AND NOTES

- Give just one "How to" to each group and have them present an answer in 1 minute or less.

- Video or audio record the presentations and review them later.

- Ask each group of delegates to create a "How to" and then swap these with another group to answer.

How To's

▶ Suggest some solutions to the following

▶ How to ....

▶ How to ....

FLIP 18

Iceberg Chart

APPLICATION

"Iceberg" thinking is a useful way of analysing problems and issues. It looks at any situation knowing that most of the situation is not immediately obvious, or visible.

This is a useful activity to develop a practical approach to finalising problems. It can be used in a variety of topics, and at any time during a training course.

PROCEDURE

- ☑ Draw the suggested iceberg illustration on a flip chart. Perhaps work through an example by writing a problem or issue in the top part, i.e. visible, section of the iceberg and then ask delegates to suggest possible causes or contributing factors happening underneath the surface. For example, mistakes being made could be the problem, and underlying causes may include such things as poor morale, lack of proper systems, no formal quality checks, no written procedures, poor quality products from suppliers, unrealistic deadlines, or no accountability.

- ☑ Prior to the training course identify an issue that you would like the group to address or analyse as part of their training activities. Alternatively, this could be something that has arisen during the training.

- ☑ Form the delegates into syndicates of 4-7 people and give them the task of analysing the underlying issues and causes that relate to the problem or situation that you have given them.

- ☑ Ask each group to present back to the main group, preparing their own flip chart page.

- ☑ Distribute flip chart paper and pens as required to individual syndicates.

- ☑ Allow 15 - 20 minutes.

- ☑ Ask each group to present back.

RELATED FLIP CHARTS

Brainstorming, Driving Forces, Team Solutions

Iceberg Chart

▶ Problems are like icebergs – you only see part on the surface, but there are many causes and issues underlying them

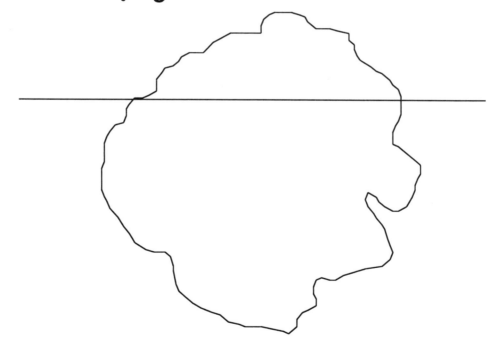

VARIATIONS AND NOTES

- ☑ Instead of you selecting a problem or issue, ask each syndicate to select a significant problem or difficulty that they face in *their* work. Once each syndicate has agreed on such a topic, ask them to take the 15 - 20 minutes to discuss the issues underlying the problem.

- ☑ Instead of giving one issue to all the syndicates, give different situations or issues to each different syndicate. In this way a range of different problems or challenges can be addressed.

- ☑ Once the underlying causes and issues have been identified, ask delegates to re-form into their syndicates and suggest ways to overcome or prevent some of the underlying causes occurring or to reduce their effect. In this way the problem or issue can be tackled at source.

- ☑ Run a short discussion after each presentation. This discussion should further expand any key terms or phrases to really establish clear definitions of what the underlying issues or causes might be.

If I Were ...

APPLICATION

This is an interesting ice-breaker or energiser that has people looking at things from a different perspective. It can be used in all sorts of training topics - safety, sales, customer service, management skills, etc.

It has been said that what you see depends on where you sit, i.e. your view of something is purely subjective. By looking at something from another perspective you can often see it differently from the way you currently see it.

For example, recently promoted managers will often become much more appreciative of some of the financial controls and methods of working that they previously could not understand. On a personal note, people often say that becoming a parent changes their perspective simply because of the new role in which they operate.

PROCEDURE

- ☑ Transfer the suggested points to a flip chart page in order to introduce and explain the exercise.

- ☑ Either select or have delegates select a typical situation that they may find themselves in. For example, dealing with an angry or difficult customer, enforcing safety standards, explaining computer procedures, and so on.

- ☑ Select or ask delegates to pick a person, role or personality from which to view a particular situation or issue, e.g. "If I were a Customer/Managing Director/ Space Alien/Prime Minister ..."

- ☑ Form delegates into pairs or small groups and ask them to list things that they would change or implement, etc on a flip chart page.

- ☑ Encourage delegates to see things differently through the eyes of their new role. For example, take the side of being a customer when resolving a situation or issue of your organisation. Does it look different when trying to find a solution if you are the customer or the customer service person?

- ☑ Post pages around the room and review each in turn.

If I Were ...

▶ Select a significant person or personality, real or fictional, dead or alive

▶ Identify a situation you find challenging

▶ Discuss and note how this person would handle it

FLIP 20

RELATED FLIP CHARTS

My Secret.

VARIATIONS AND NOTES

☑ Ask delegates to take the opposite position or role to the role they are playing. For example, if they are a Safety Officer have them take the role or position of an operative whom they are trying to convince to work more safety. If they are an operative or individual have them take the position of somebody who has been injured due to their lack of care or negligence. If they are a policeman have them take the role of a criminal or suspect, if they are a teacher have them take the role of a pupil, if a manager have them take the role of one of their members of staff.

☑ In advance of the training prepare a set of 3 inch x 5 inch cards with pre-determined situations and pre-determined characters on and give out these cards one from each pile or each set to each of the pairs or small groups.

I Wish I Had

APPLICATION

It is often said that we do not regret the things we do, we regret the things that we don't do. This exercise asks delegates to apply that kind of thinking to themselves and their own personal lives.

It asks delegates to consider which things will they wish they had done now when they are 75 or 80 years old if they continue in the same way. Will they look back at this time and think of things that they wish they had done, maybe learning a musical instrument, for example, or spending more or less time doing certain things in their lives?

This is a useful exercise in helping identify goals and areas of personal development.

PROCEDURE

- Draw the suggested points and illustration onto a flip chart page.

- Explain that we all have things that we wish we had done. Some are very minor and some more important.

- Distribute flip chart paper and pens to delegates.

- Ask trainees to think of "wish I had's" that they might still be able to work on e.g. travelling abroad, learning how to swim, etc.

- They should draw or write each of these "I wish I had's" graphically on a flip chart.

- Ask each person in turn to identify their "wish I had's" and then to explain why they are important to them and how they might achieve them.

- Allow 10 - 15 minutes for delegates to complete their flip chart pages.

- Run a short discussion around the key themes asking delegates - what is stopping them doing some of these things now?

I Wish I Had

▶ Imagine yourself aged 75 or 80

▶ What things do you wish you had done in your life?

FLIP 21

RELATED FLIP CHARTS

Goal Setting.

VARIATIONS AND NOTES

- ☑ Instead of asking delegates to consider things they would have wished they had done when they look back at the age of 75 or 80 years, ask them to consider what they would change about their life looking back knowing what they now know. This will sometimes highlight routines or working patterns that are not ideal but, if left, will perpetuate.

- ☑ Expand the discussion following the exercise and ask delegates to consider the things that they think they wish they had done, the things they want to achieve or things they ought to do. Why not start doing them now on the basis that it is never really too late, except when it is really too late!

- ☑ Once delegates have presented back their "I wish I had"s, group them together in terms of similar "wishes". For example, those that said that they wish they had spent more time at home and less time working could form one group, those that wish they had learnt a new sport or skill could form another group. Those that wish they had continued their education and learnt new languages or knowledge would form another group. Then allow each group 15 - 20 minutes to discuss how they could actually move forward in trying to achieve or change their lives in the ways they have identified.

Jargon Jumble

APPLICATION

A good exercise to introduce or review key terms or jargon related to a topic (e.g. computer terms).

It is based on the principle that virtually every area or expertise, knowledge or profession has associated with it a large amount of proprietary jargon. For example, solicitors, medical practitioners, even pizza chefs have their own particular terms and expressions which are meaningless to the outsider. Often even people within these professions have vague understandings of what each of these terms are and perhaps do not fully understand where the expressions originate from. For example, we might all talk about computer RAM but not recognise what the initials stand for or exactly what it is.

This exercise can be used in two ways, either at the beginning of a training course as a way of introducing key terms, phrases and knowledge, or at the end of a training session to review some of the terms and expressions that have been used to reinforce the understanding and to test comprehension.

PROCEDURE

- ☑ In advance of the training, develop a list of about 12 key pieces of jargon or technical terms related to the topic that you are training.

- ☑ Write up the flip chart page(s) with as many examples of jargon as you wish.

- ☑ Either go around the room or ask for volunteers. Ask each trainee in turn to stand up, pick a word/phrase and state the definition.

- ☑ If it is correct, tick it off and move onto the next person. If not, ask somebody else to offer an alternative or correct definition.

RELATED FLIP CHARTS

Keyword Summary, Anagram Quiz, Quick Quiz, Six Point Profile and Jigsaw.

Jargon Jumble

▶ When asked, give a definition for the following terms:

VARIATIONS AND NOTES

- ☑ Form delegates into two teams and ask each team to list 12 pieces of jargon or 12 technical terms from the topic or course. Have them then swap papers and give them five minutes to write as many definitions as they can against each term.

- ☑ When all definitions have been guessed correctly, review the terms on the chart and discuss where the terms originated from or whether their meanings are fully explained.

Jigsaw Summary

APPLICATION

This is an unusual way of summarising the content from a training course or a training session. It gathers together relevant information under key headings, each provided by a different pair or syndicate within the main group.

PROCEDURE

- ☑ Draw or prepare the suggested flip chart page and display to the group. Explain the process - that each group will be working on one single aspect of the course - and then put together a montage to cover the course in its entirety.

- ☑ Divide the main group into pairs or syndicates.

- ☑ Give each team or pair one element or a single topic from the training course.

- ☑ They should then summarise all the main points from this topic only on a flip chart page.

- ☑ Distribute flip chart paper and pens to each team or pair.

- ☑ Encourage delegates to put down anything at all that they can think of about the element or topic that they are depicting - diagrams, quotes, models, phrases, drawings, bullet points and so on.

- ☑ Allow 10 - 15 minutes.

- ☑ Arrange the pages in a logical sequence to form a whole.

- ☑ Re-convene the group and invite others to add any missing or additional points to any page.

RELATED FLIP CHARTS

Mind Map, Top Ten Ideas, Keyword Summary.

Jigsaw Summary

▶ Work on one aspect of today's topic ONLY

▶ Write everything you can think of about this on a page

▶ Display in a montage or mural

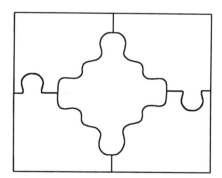

VARIATIONS AND NOTES

☑ Instead of giving each group 10 - 15 minutes for one topic, set a time limit of 5 minutes and then ask each group to pass their flip chart page to the group or pair to their left, then spending five minutes adding additional points or observations that the other group may have missed. This can be repeated two or three times.

Keyword Summary

APPLICATION

This is a good exercise to energise a group and review key concepts or learning points.

The exercise was inspired by the radio programme "Just a Minute". In this programme contestants have to talk for a minute on a given topic without repetition, hesitation or deviation. Whilst this may sound fairly simple, it is actually very difficult to do, and often produces much hilarity in the attempt.

PROCEDURE

- ☑ On the flip chart draw or write keywords or key subject headings from the training session. Make sure there are as many words as delegates.

- ☑ Next, go around the group in sequence or at random as follows:

- ☑ when selected, a person should stand up and talk for 1 minute without repeating themselves or pausing (should they repeat themselves or falter, they must sit down or stop and hand over to somebody else).

- ☑ NB: You need to listen carefully for these pauses and repetitions.

- ☑ Continue until all words have been covered.

RELATED FLIP CHARTS

Jigsaw Summary, Jargon Jumble.

Keyword Summary

▶ When asked, talk about one of the topics below for one minute, without pause or repetition

FLIP 24

VARIATIONS AND NOTES

- ☑ Instead of you setting the topics, divide delegates into different teams and have them set topics for each other.

- ☑ Invite delegates to challenge the speaker at any time.

- ☑ Perhaps you might like to record each presentation and then review them to see if the people are actually speaking sense or just making something up as they go along.

- ☑ Ask delegates to then take a moment to prepare a one minute presentation on a key term or learning point and see if they can do a better job having taken time to prepare in advance.

Keys to Success

APPLICATION

This can be used to summarise and review learning elements or key points at the end of a training course or session.

The thinking behind this exercise is that delegates often will focus on three or four main key learning points following any training session. This is not to say that the other learning points in the training session have not made an impact or will not be implemented, it is certainly the case that many ideas and thoughts from a training programme can stay with people for many years. However, in the immediate days and weeks following a training programme, there will probably be three or four key ideas or changes that they will focus on the most.

This exercise asks delegates to consider what those might be.

PROCEDURE

- ☑ Draw the following on a flip chart writing the theme or topic at the bottom or top of the page.

- ☑ Ask delegates to work in groups to summarise the essential and most important elements, or things to be done to ensure success.

- ☑ Ask delegates to keep their points to one page of flip chart paper and limit their presentation to one minute or less.

- ☑ Distribute flip chart paper and pens to each group.

- ☑ Allow 10 - 15 minutes for preparation asking each group to present in teams.

Keys to Success

▶ Summarise the most essential points from the course in some easy-to-remember phrases or paragraphs

FLIP 25

RELATED FLIP CHARTS

Jigsaw Summary, Keyword Summary, Jargon Jumble, Action Plan, Billboard, Do's and Don'ts.

VARIATIONS AND NOTES

- ☑ Ask delegates to prepare individually, not just in groups.

- ☑ As well as listing key elements, stress that delegates should put these in order of priority.

- ☑ Ask delegates to take a copy of their own personal key to success and then review them with their manager following the programme.

- ☑ Have delegates work individually for 5-10 minutes developing their own "keys to success" list and then discuss them within a group or team.

Metaphors

APPLICATION

Educators often note that the education system tends to over-develop the left side of the brain during the important years of 12 to 16, often diminishing our ability to think with our right brain. This is emphasised by simple examples, for instance, consider how many hours you may have spent learning English, Maths and technical subjects, perhaps at the expense of subjects such as Art, Music or Poetry. One interesting example of this is to display a piece of modern art, perhaps an abstract painting. Ask the group to consider the painting and suggest what they think it may mean. A proportion of any group will probably highlight it as a lot of nonsense saying they cannot see anything at all.

This is an unusual and interesting exercise to generate creativity and alternative thinking.

PROCEDURE

- ☑ Introduce the whole exercise by asking the group to consider some common metaphors that they use, perhaps unconsciously. Consider these expressions: "I'm running out of time", "I can give you five minutes". These relate to time as being a fixed tangible commodity. It suggests it is something we can cut up and package.

- ☑ Draw the suggested (metaphor) picture, or another of your choice, on a flip chart.

- ☑ Ask delegates to consider what they think or what meaning they would assign to the illustration of a man reaching for a carrot suspended from a stick over his head, as per the flip chart page. What does it mean to them? Answers might include, self-motivation, setting goals for yourself which are unattainable, striving for something which is out of reach.

- ☑ Next select a topic or focus (e.g. "my career", "self-development", "our organisation", "being a manager").

Metaphors

▶ Describe a metaphor to summarise, illustrate or express your thoughts about a key element from today's course

FLIP 26

- ☑ Ask delegates to think of and draw or describe their thoughts and feelings about the chosen topic or theme in the form of a metaphor, for example they might see their organisation as a cliff face. Being a manager might be like being a television set constantly trying to tune in to different channels and flicking from one channel to another in desperation.

- ☑ Allow 15 - 20 minutes.

- ☑ Display around the room and discuss.

RELATED FLIP CHARTS

Mind Map, My Favourite, Team Talents.

VARIATIONS AND NOTES

- ☑ Brainstorm or discuss with colleagues metaphors that they may think of or consider appropriate in their lives or work. For example, discuss what metaphors they might use to describe their role as a trainer. This can give you some useful and relevant examples in order to introduce the exercise.

- ☑ Ask delegates to consider how they view the element that they are looking at by changing the metaphor they are using. For example, if they use a metaphor of a river to discuss or relate to their career flowing from one position to another, constantly meandering, how does this change when they consider a different metaphor such as a farmer, cultivating and developing things around them?

Mind Map

APPLICATION

Mind mapping is a way of notating ideas or thoughts that is markedly different from using logical or lateral thinking. Instead of listing things in a sequence, typically from the top to the bottom of a page, mind mapping allows ideas to literally flow in a lateral or completely non-logical sequence around the page.

A mind map can also incorporate such things as pictures, icons and different colours to notate different meanings or themes. For example, if you are mind mapping a topic such as Hollywood you would write the word "Hollywood" in the middle of a page then allow your thoughts to develop to say Clint Eastwood, then think of spaghetti because of spaghetti westerns, drawing a branch off showing a plateful of spaghetti.

As bizarre as this may sound, research and experiments have shown that using mind mapping can aid recall and comprehension.

This activity can be used in a variety of ways to map existing views and knowledge at the start of a course; examine issues or problems or to summarise at the end of session. (For more information on mind mapping see books by Edward de Bono and Tony Buzan, amongst others.)

PROCEDURE

- ☑ Draw an example mind map on a flip chart in advance, remembering that a mind map might contain different colours, pictures and icons. Use other examples, why not do your own mind map?

- ☑ Review the elements of a mind map and the rationale behind it (i.e. allows lateral thinking and the free flow of ideas).

- ☑ Select an issue and form delegates into small groups or pairs to work on it.

- ☑ Allow 15 - 20 minutes.

- ☑ Display pages around the room and ask delegates to circulate and to review the maps.

Mind Map

▶ Draw a mind map, letting your ideas flow as they come to you

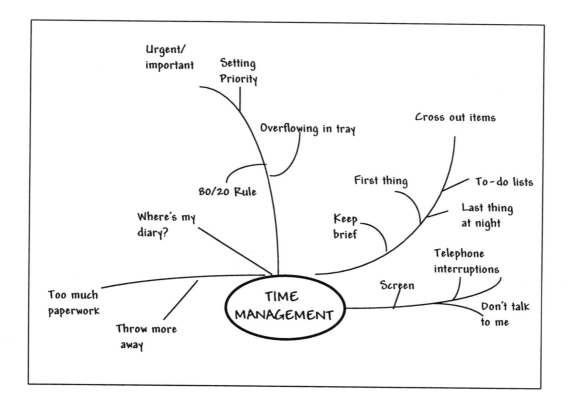

FLIP 27

RELATED FLIP CHARTS

Brainstorming, Flowcharting, Driving Forces, Change Planner, Cartoon Time, Jigsaw Summary.

VARIATIONS AND NOTES

- ☑ Why not introduce the idea of mind mapping right at the start of your training course and then at regular intervals, say once an hour. Direct delegates to go back to their mind map and add additional elements to summarise the points or ideas that have just been covered. In this way the mind map will actually build up and develop during the training course.

- ☑ At the end of a session take more time and allow the delegates to fine-tune their mind map before displaying it and presenting the best to the group.

- ☑ After five minutes of the individual syndicates or groups working on their mind map, have them stop and rotate their positions, leaving the mind maps they are working on the tables in place. They will then continue working on somebody else's mind map. In this way certain words and ideas might cross-fertilise.

Mnemonic Challenge

APPLICATION

This exercise is an interesting way of reviewing and summarising at the end of a presentation or training session.

Mnemonics have been identified as interesting ways to remember and review information.

PROCEDURE

- ☑ Write an example mnemonic on the flip chart.

- ☑ Explain that a mnemonic, apart from being an intriguing mental puzzle to invent, acts as a useful memory hook e.g. using a memorable date, Christmas Day, as the house alarm number, 2512.

- ☑ Form delegates into pairs or small groups and ask them to select a word associated with, or related to, the training topic and create a mnemonic that contains key points. Transfer to flip pages. The mnemonic could be a word, the letters of which can be used as the initial letters of words associated with the training course or the key word. For example, B-Safe is more memorable than Be Safe.

- ☑ Distribute flip chart paper and pens.

- ☑ Display pages around the room, offer a prize for the best one.

- ☑ Timing allow 10 - 15 minutes.

RELATED FLIP CHARTS

Jargon Jungle, Jigsaw Summary, Six Point Profile, Quick Quiz.

Mnemonic Challenge

▶ Create a mnemonic which is relevant to and contains some ideas from the course.

F
U
N

Flip chart
Universal
Notes

FLIP 28

VARIATIONS AND NOTES

- ☑ Perhaps experiment with giving groups different words to see if they can make other mnemonics. Ask delegates to share any mnemonics they have invented and used in personal, family or study situations.

- ☑ If you are running a number of courses on the same or similar topic you could build up a collection of different mnemonics to share with the group and actually integrate with your training material.

My Secret

APPLICATION

A good ice-breaker or session starter for any course or meeting.

This activity is a good way to start a session, particularly where people may know each other and traditional ice-breakers are not really relevant. It can also be good in building teams of people and encouraging them to share information about each other in an informal, light-hearted and non-threatening manner.

PROCEDURE

- ☑ Ask delegates to write down on a piece of paper something that nobody else in the room knows about them. (Perhaps include one yourself.)

- ☑ Collect all the papers and shuffle. One at a time read out the secret and write one word to summarise it on the flip chart.

- ☑ The rest of the group has to try and guess who is the owner of the secret.

- ☑ Write the owner of the secret against each.

- ☑ Continue until all secrets are revealed.

RELATED FLIP CHARTS

Team Talents, My Favourite.

VARIATIONS AND NOTES

- ☑ You might want to include one or two red herrings that do not belong to anybody just to try and get people thinking.

- ☑ You could give the exercise a different focus by asking delegates to write down what is a secret but maybe embarrassing moment, or some confession that they have done something in the past and got away with it (of a minor nature hopefully!).

- ☑ Another variation of this exercise is to ask the group to write down one phrase or expression that was used to describe them in a school report. Put the pieces of paper, each one containing the expression or phrase, together, jumble them up and see if the delegates can guess which phrase relates to each person.

My Secret

▶ Write down on a piece of paper one thing that nobody else in the room knows about you!

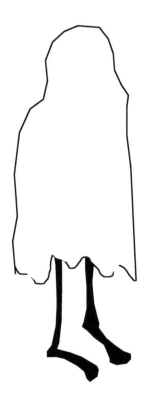

FLIP 29

My Favourite

APPLICATION

A useful, entertaining and often revealing ice-breaker.

PROCEDURE

- ☑ Write (perhaps with illustrations) a selection of categories on a flip chart page.

- ☑ Ask each delegate to take two and a half minutes to write down quickly their "favourite" example. If they can't think of a favourite, write down the first thing that comes to mind.

- ☑ Go around the group reviewing one person at a time.

- ☑ Offer your own if you wish.

- ☑ Conduct an overall résumé mentioning how the range of choices illustrates the range of individual preferences in any group.

RELATED FLIP CHARTS

My Secret, Team Talents, If I Were …

VARIATIONS AND NOTES

- ☑ There is, in fact, an endless list of categories that you could use for this exercise. Obviously such things as cars, films, books, plays, food are the most obvious. Why not try ways of relaxing, sport, board games?

- ☑ If you run this exercise at one session in a course, later run its opposite, "My Least Favourite", asking delegates to identify their least-liked example of the categories.

- ☑ Over several training courses build a collection of these to see if there are any top 10s that you can deduce.

My Favourite

▶ In a few minutes, write down your favourite of each of the following categories (or the first example that comes in to your mind)

eg: Car
     Film
     Book
     Play
     Food
     Colour
     Activity
     Place
     Holiday
     City

Next Steps

APPLICATION

A good end of session activity to facilitate and develop practical action plans. A variation on the Action Plan theme. Instead of asking delegates to consider setting goals or objectives, which may not be applicable to certain courses, this exercise simply asks delegates to identify what are the key "Next Steps". It can be particularly useful after any short training session, meeting or team discussion where it is important to summarise what has been discussed, and agreed, prior to the group departing.

PROCEDURE

- ☑ After summarising the key points from the course or session, illustrate them on a flip chart page.

- ☑ Form delegates into pairs or small groups.

- ☑ Supply flip chart paper and pens.

- ☑ Set them the task, "Identify the initial or next steps in implementing or applying ideas from the training session".

- ☑ Allow 15 minutes.

- ☑ Ask each group in turn to present their plans.

RELATED FLIP CHARTS

Action Plan, Goal Setting.

VARIATIONS AND NOTES

- ☑ Have delegates draw their next steps as the illustration of a staircase or ladder, giving a priority or sequence to the events.

- ☑ Encourage the next steps to be clear and specific in terms of how they are going to be implemented.

- ☑ After each group has presented their plans run a discussion to see if it is possible to arrive at a plan of the most important next steps.

Next Steps

▶ Identify the initial or next steps to implement ideas and changes from today

FLIP 31

Nicknames

APPLICATION

It is interesting to observe that most of us at one time have had a nickname, most probably when we were at school. Sometimes you will find that people have nicknames that their partner uses or their close friends outside of work. This exercise allows people to share personal non-threatening information in perhaps a fun and informal manner, learning more about other team members.

It is also useful to use with a group where people know each other quite well, and traditional ice-breakers would not perhaps be appropriate.

This is a lively and amusing ice-breaker and group energiser.

PROCEDURE

- Ask delegates to write down a nickname they have had or would like to have, past or present.
- Ask them to fold this paper up and pass to you.
- Next write all the names on a flip chart page.
- Finally, quiz the group to guess who owns the nickname.
- The whole exercise should take about 10 - 15 minutes

RELATED FLIP CHARTS

My Favourite, My Secret, This is Me, If I Were ....

VARIATIONS AND NOTES

- Ask people to invent a nickname for themselves.
- Do they know of any people, past or present, who have unusual nicknames. This makes an interesting discussion.
- Does anybody use a "handle" in any work that they do, such as radio communication, C.B, e-mail, Internet etc.

Nicknames

▶ Can you match the nickname (past or present) to the people in the room?

Flower

Trigger

Daisy

Sugar

Dobbin

BUSTER

FLIP 32

Old Habits To New

APPLICATION

Any skills-based training course such as time management, customer service, communication skills, interviewing and so on may have the goal of improving levels of behaviour on a day to day basis for the individuals on the training.

This exercise looks at the skills and knowledge learnt on a course and translates it into personal behaviours or habits. It notes that most of us operate for much of the day on an unconscious automatic pilot level. These unconscious habits allow us to do things without very much conscious thought. However, they also mean that sometimes we build bad habits into things we are doing, for example, driving.

A useful exercise for any personal development or skill-based training session or programme.

PROCEDURE

- ☑ Draw the "table" overleaf on a flip chart page.

- ☑ Form delegates into small groups or pairs.

- ☑ Set them the task of first identifying three bad or less than effective behaviours, routines or habits that they would like to change.

- ☑ Distribute flip chart paper and pens to delegates.

- ☑ Next complete the box "New Habits" with the behaviour that might replace it.

- ☑ Finally, identify some practical ideas on how to achieve this.

- ☑ Discuss an example that the group can relate to such as driving, managing meetings, using the computer.

RELATED FLIP CHARTS

Next Steps, Action Plan, Driving Forces.

Old Habits To New

▶ Identify 3 behaviours or habits that you would like to change, and what the NEW habits would be.

Old Habits	New Habits

FLIP 33

VARIATIONS AND NOTES

☑ During the training course be alert to the objectives and discussions going on during the different sessions and create your own list of bad habits or bad practices that delegates refer to during the sessions. Keep this list to one side and then produce it and ask delegates to review it in this exercise.

☑ If you conducted a pre-training analysis this may have identified the key areas of improvement.

Parking Lot

APPLICATION

This can be used during the course to post any issues questions, observations, concerns etc, about the subject under discussion or related topics.

In any training course issues can be raised which are outside the scope of either the trainer's jurisdiction or the content of the course. There may be things that are specific to an individual's relationship with their manager or perhaps to do with the organisation's policies or procedures, or even politics.

In order to avoid issues interrupting the course or impacting on the trainer's credibility in handling them, this mechanism is a useful way of catching these positively and then moving on to focus on the training issues at hand.

PROCEDURE

- ☑ The exercise is best set up and described within the first few minutes of the training course, perhaps when you are running through the logistics and course timing. Take a piece of flip chart paper and divide it into a parking lot. Review and summarise at the end of the course or at some point following it.

- ☑ Draw the illustration overleaf on a flip chart.

- ☑ Post the page at the side or back of the room, or perhaps next to the coffee station.

- ☑ Distribute some post-it note pads amongst the delegates.

- ☑ Explain that if they have any points that come to mind on any aspect of the course content to write them on a post-it note and stick on the parking lot during an appropriate break.

- ☑ Review at regular intervals during the day.

RELATED FLIP CHARTS

Problem Graffiti, Brainstorming.

Parking Lot

▶ Please park your issues, questions, concerns or queries here.

FLIP 34

VARIATIONS AND NOTES

- ☑ Your review session can discuss each of the post-its on the parking lot and group them together, perhaps re-wording them into two or three clear issues that are coming up.

- ☑ Following the training, write a short note to the delegates referring back to the issues on the parking lot and explaining your procedure in dealing with them.

- ☑ If the training is an on-going process, review the process of dealing with these issues at a subsequent training event.

Pictogram

APPLICATION

Instead of the traditional word-based end of course or end of meeting summaries, this is an alternative approach.

A good exercise to summarise a course or individual session.

PROCEDURE

- ☑ Draw a simple example on a flip chart, for instance if you are running a safety course draw an illustration of somebody lifting something carefully with arrow and notations showing the correct techniques being used. On the other hand, if you are running a computer training course, show the picture of a computer or a typical screen with arrows pointing to the different elements.

- ☑ Introduce the exercise by highlighting that often people remember things that they associate with pictures, not just with words. For example, how many people remember someone's face, but often forget their name?

- ☑ Explain that this exercise asks people to think visually and to choose or create a picture icon or graphic of some kind that will allow them to summarise and remember the key elements of the course.

- ☑ Form delegates into small groups.

- ☑ Discuss one or two examples.

- ☑ Give each group a blank flip chart page with some illustrations or pictures to summarise what has just been covered. Ask them to consider which are the most important planning points for the training course.

- ☑ Have the delegates discuss ideas as to how to represent these points visually or pictorially, perhaps using a diagram, cartoon, icons or pictures.

- ☑ This should take about 15 - 20 minutes.

- ☑ Post around the room and review.

Pictogram

▶ Summarise one or more key points from the course using pictures, icons or graphics.

RELATED FLIP CHARTS

Old Habits To New, Action Plan, Six Point Profile, Jigsaw Summary.

VARIATIONS AND NOTES

- ☑ Have delegates work on a type of picture or graphic that you give them. For example you may give one group the task of summarising the course content based around the London Underground tube system. Another might do it as a newspaper cartoon, with somebody else doing it as a series of Internet or computer style icons.

Priority Matrix

APPLICATION

This exercise can be used to illustrate how to set priorities. It is ideal for any time management or similar type of training programme. It can be used successfully on other types of courses, for example, security training, team building, project planning and perhaps even quality management.

The essence of any priority is its relevant importance and its relevant urgency. Once these are identified the priority can be positioned relative to all the other tasks or activities that we may need to consider.

Another exercise would be when delegates are considering the Action Plan at the end of a course, they could then prioritise the events that they intend to schedule.

PROCEDURE

- ☑ Explain that a priority has two basic fundamental principles; importance and urgency. Discuss some relevant examples. Draw delegates' attention to the fact that sometimes we mistake what is most urgent as being of high priority when really it should be what is most important. Discuss the tendency to put off important but not urgent tasks until they are both important and urgent. For example, revising for an exam, buying Christmas presents, doing a report or expenses form. Highlight the benefit of planning properly and setting priorities in advance.

- ☑ Draw and explain the priority matrix and the key principles of making time for what is most important, not just the most urgent or enjoyable tasks.

- ☑ Have delegates make a list of ten or more activities or tasks they want to schedule or complete in the next seven to ten days. They can be either work or personal items, but try and break down the big tasks into component activities. Make sure they have on the list such things as telephone calls, letters, faxes, meetings, appointments, activities, and things to do. Once a list has been completed for each delegate, ask them to draw two columns on the right-hand side of the page. At the top of one column write the word IMPORTANT and of the second column the word URGENT. Now ask them to rank each item from their "To Do" list as 1-10 for importance, 10 being the most important and 1 being the least, and 1-10 for urgency (10 will be very urgent and 1 not urgent at all).

Priority Matrix

▶ Decide on how important things are and how urgent. This is the key to setting priorities.

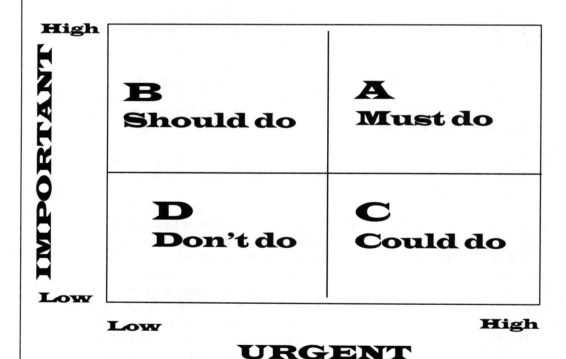

FLIP 36

- ☑ When the delegates have completed this, ask them to take a piece of flip chart paper and transfer their tasks and activities onto the corresponding rating on the matrix. For example, if a particular task was rated as an 8 for importance but only a 3 for urgent, then it would sit in quadrant B. Ask them to continue until all the tasks and activities are allocated into a quadrant or box on the matrix.

- ☑ When this is done, explain the different ways of scheduling each collection of activities. For example, anything in box A is both urgent and important and needs to be done first. Anything in box B is important but not urgent and time needs to be scheduled or in some way set aside to achieve these things before they become urgent. Anything in box C is a possible action to do if we have the time. More commonly elements in boxes C and D need to be discarded, delegated or deferred.

- ☑ Supply flip chart paper and pens.

- ☑ Ask delegates to apply this model to actions and "To Do's" they may have; rating each on the 1 - 10 scales and the plotting on the matrix.

- ☑ Allow 15 minutes or as required.

- ☑ Go around the group reviewing examples.

RELATED FLIP CHARTS

Action Plan, Flowcharting, Criteria Grid, Change Planner.

VARIATIONS AND NOTES

- ☑ Instead of having delegates make a list of their own tasks and activities, have one previously prepared and ask them to assess the relative importance and urgency of each task.

- ☑ Instead of using the numbers 1-10, it is simpler to set classifications as being high or low.

Problem-solving Graffiti

APPLICATION

This is a good exercise to tackle problems or obstacles highlighted during, or as part of, a training course.

It can be used at any time during the training course, meeting or event and is good to get delegates up and moving around.

PROCEDURE

- ☑ First, either during pre-course preparation or during the training event, list a series of common problems or issues that you feel (or the delegates have expressed that) they experience.

- ☑ Write one issue or problem at the top of a separate flip chart page (or invite delegates to generate these).

- ☑ Post pages evenly around the room (several different pages can be posted up at once).

- ☑ Invite trainees to circulate around the room and write some positive graffiti on each page. These should be hints, tips, ideas or solutions to the problem.

- ☑ Allow 15 minutes.

- ☑ Review each page in turn.

RELATED FLIP CHARTS

Brainstorming, Billboard, Team Solutions, Iceberg Chart.

Problem-solving Graffiti

▶ Circulate around the room writing graffiti solutions on all of the charts.

My Boss

Communication

Approach

Talk

Meetings

FLIP 37

Variations and Notes

☑ Give each pair or small group of delegates a flip chart page and ask them to consider a problem or issue and write that in the middle of the page. Each group must then post their page on the wall before circulating around giving thought to solutions of other problems.

☑ Another way of running this exercise is to form the group into small syndicates or teams and have them spend three minutes in front of each problem flip chart page scribbling up ideas, solutions, suggestions, tips etc before moving on (when the whole room moves on) to the next flip chart.

☑ At the end of this exercise collect in the flip chart pages and then have them summarised or reviewed later.

Puzzle Phrases (Rebuses)

APPLICATION

An intriguing and light-hearted way of starting and finishing any session.

This type of brainteaser has been a popular ice-breaker for training courses and meetings for some time.

This collection of puzzles has been selected because of the ease with which they can be drawn on a flip chart page. You can use them in a formal way by putting up four or five at a time, or simply in between sessions or different topics.

PROCEDURE

- ☑ Draw one or more "Puzzles" on to a flip chart page.

- ☑ Invite delegates to guess a well-known phrase or saying that each might represent.

- ☑ See Appendix for examples and solutions.

- ☑ Option: Ask delegates to invent some of their own to test the group.

- ☑ The example is "High Income Bracket".

RELATED FLIP CHARTS

Cartoon Time, Billboard, Metaphors, Quick Quiz.

Puzzle Phrases

Income

VARIATIONS AND NOTES

- ☑ As a variation, after running the exercise once or twice during a session, task delegates with designing or creating their own puzzles for the rest of the group to guess.

- ☑ Start off with some of the easier puzzles and work through to some of the more difficult ones, leaving these open from one session to another giving a longer time to solve.

Quick Quiz

Application

A noisy and enjoyable way of summarising or ending the training course or session.

This activity can save a trainer or facilitator a great deal of time in preparation, and in some ways is even more effective than having a prepared training quiz. Delegates will review the training material or course content both in the creation of the quiz and again when they try to answer questions.

Either way it is very good for reviewing and summarising the key points from any session.

Procedure

- First divide the group into two teams on opposite sides of the room.

- Write the instructions on a flip chart page.

- Ask each team to take 10 minutes to create questions.

- When each team has a list of questions, you need to act as Quiz Master, alternating the questions from one team or group to another. Use the flip chart to keep score as the teams go through, scoring two points for a correct answer and one for a half correct answer.

- Set the quiz session going, delegates quizzing each other in pairs or syndicates.

- Allow 20 - 25 minutes.

Related Flip Charts

Puzzle Phrases (Rebuses), Anagram Quiz.

Quick Quiz

▶ Work in pairs

▶ Each person lists ten questions based on the course

▶ Take turns to ask questions; keep score

1
2
3
4
5
6
7
8
9
10

VARIATIONS AND NOTES

- ☑ Instead of running the quiz in two teams, ask delegates to write down questions individually and then quiz each other, working in pairs.

- ☑ For a shorter quiz session, to review an individual module or section of a course, simply aim to have three questions rather than ten.

- ☑ Have some questions of your own prepared, of a general nature, which you could throw in as tie-breakers.

- ☑ Circulate among the teams or delegates and encourage them to have different types of questions, such things as missing words, multiple choice, explanations etc.

Reasons to Learn

APPLICATION

This exercise should be used at the start of a training course or session to emphasise the potential benefits and importance of the subject.

PROCEDURE

- ☑ Draw the two columns on flip chart pages or one page for each.

- ☑ Explain that this exercise will ask delegates to consider what is the value in the training or topic that they are about to take part in. It will ask them to consider what they will gain, what benefits and what value from improving their skills and knowledge in a particular area, and also what the consequences will be of not learning new skills and improving themselves in this way.

- ☑ Distribute flip chart paper and pens.

- ☑ Ask delegates to work in twos or threes and highlight "benefits" and "consequences" of being mediocre or less skilled.

- ☑ Allow 10 - 15 minutes.

- ☑ Post pages around the room and review.

RELATED FLIP CHARTS

Hopes and Concerns, Driving Forces, Old Habits To New.

VARIATIONS AND NOTES

- ☑ After introducing and explaining the exercise, ask delegates to write down one benefit and one consequence. Allow 1-2 minutes.

- ☑ When this is done, go around the room and ask each delegate to read out their notes, or their benefit and their consequence, and summarise them collectively on a flip chart at the front of the group.

Reasons to Learn

▶ Consider the <u>benefits</u> of doing things well, and the <u>consequences</u> of poor performance

FLIP 40

Say It Another Way

APPLICATION

Suitable for any training course where good, clear and positive communication is important e.g. customer service, people management, telephone skills, etc.

During our daily work and lives we may use many expressions over and over again. Because of their familiarity the sincerity and meaning is lost and the phrases can come across as sounding hollow and insincere. For example, how many times have you heard someone say "Hold please" or "Sorry to keep you waiting"? We need to try and think about identifying these phrases and convert them into more positive alternatives. This is the purpose of this exercise.

PROCEDURE

- ☑ Draw on a flip chart some relevant examples of "Common Phrases" and sayings.

- ☑ Typical examples could be taken from the following, "They are in a meeting", "Hold please", "Company policy is …", etc. Discuss what might be different ways of saying these things in a more positive or user friendly way.

- ☑ Form delegates into small groups or pairs and ask them to first give ten examples of unhelpful or not very good phrases, excuses etc, and list them on their own flip chart page and suggest better alternatives.

- ☑ If needed give delegates a context for the phrases, for example, phrases that people use on the telephone or in and around the office, or maybe when they are being served as customers, computer jargon or technical terms.

- ☑ Allow 10 - 15 minutes.

- ☑ Post pages around the room and discuss different examples.

RELATED FLIP CHARTS

Jargon Jungle, Team Solutions.

Say It Another Way

▶ Take the words or phrases and come up with more positive alternatives

* from *"The computer's broken again"*.
* to *"I cannot access that information at the moment"*.

FLIP 41

VARIATIONS AND NOTES

☑ Prepare a list of ten or more expressions yourself relating to the course material and list these on a flip chart. Ask delegates to copy these and then give them 10 - 15 minutes to generate one positive alternative for each expression. Review in a group summary at the end.

Seven Question Summary

APPLICATION

An end of session activity that reviews and tests understanding of key points.

PROCEDURE

- ☑ Prepare a flip chart page by listing seven short questions that test either understanding or memory retention. For example, list three examples of …. How would you …?, What is the purpose of …?

- ☑ Ask trainees to answer each question, in writing.

- ☑ Review the answers and record them on the flip chart.

RELATED FLIP CHARTS

Quick Quiz, Jigsaw Summary, Keyword Summary, Keys to Success, Top Ten Ideas.

VARIATIONS AND NOTES

- ☑ Instead of picking the questions at random, tie the questions in to initial course objectives, taking the objective and turning it round into a question. For example, if one question was to learn how to insert pictures into a document, the question would then be "detail how you would insert a picture or graphic into a word processing document". This will then conclude and bring together the programme in a positive way.

- ☑ When all seven questions have been answered, task delegates with generating one additional question which they then have to read out and pick someone to answer.

Seven Question Summary

▶ Answer the following seven questions:

1
2
3
4
5
6
7

FLIP 42

Six Point Profile

APPLICATION

A good ice-breaker and group energiser. This exercise can be used equally well where delegates are known to each other or are complete strangers. It requires a level of self-disclosure which can be useful in building a team and generating an atmosphere of trust.

PROCEDURE

- ☑ Draw the text and circle overleaf onto a flip chart page.

- ☑ Distribute flip chart paper and pens.

- ☑ Post the flip chart pages around the room behind each delegate, if possible.

- ☑ Ask delegates to copy the circle onto a blank piece of paper.

- ☑ Delegates to take 10 minutes to write their responses in each slice.

- ☑ Go around the room and review each person in turn (in larger groups this can be done in syndicates).

- ☑ Conduct an overall résumé, mentioning how the range of choices illustrates the range of individual preference in any group.

RELATED FLIP CHARTS

If I Were …, Metaphors.

Six Point Profile

- 1 = Two things I do well
- 2 = One criticism - my best friend would tell me
- 3 = My personal maxim or motto
- 4 = One trait I admire in others
- 5 = One law I would change
- 6 = One person who influenced me greatly

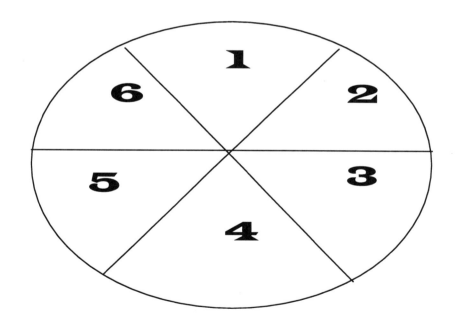

VARIATIONS AND NOTES

☑ The basic structure of the exercise can be varied enormously by simply changing the different sections or segments of the chart. For example, the topics could be varied to include such things as My Favourite Quotation, My Favourite Toy as a Child, My Favourite Toy as an Adult etc.

☑ Another variation is to have delegates do one question at different stages during the training course. For example, for the first session they would draw a circle and write in segment one two things that they do well. (It is important not to give them the following questions until the time comes for them to write them on the chart.) Later in the day give them the topic to write in segment two. This way it can be illuminating and intriguing to build up profiles during the training course, with delegates wondering what the next segment might reveal about themselves and others.

Step by Step

APPLICATION

A good activity to define, refine or review key skills, processes, procedures or operations. This is also a good exercise to develop a practised approach to solving problems.

PROCEDURE

- ☑ Draw instructions on a flip chart as overleaf. Highlight the fact that this exercise will require delegates to clarify and put into a very clear and logical sequence something they may do automatically or without any conscious thought.

- ☑ Explain that this exercise is designed to establish a thoughtful, considered and consistent approach. Select a focus/subject.

- ☑ Options are to discuss an example such as tying a tie, tying your shoelaces or something related to the training event.

- ☑ Form delegates into small groups (3 - 7 people).

- ☑ Allow 10 - 15 minutes, as required, to develop model.

- ☑ Ask each group to present their model.

- ☑ Option is to give a different topic to each group.

RELATED FLIP CHARTS

Flowcharting, Mind Map, Do's and Don'ts.

Step by Step

▶ Discuss and list a step by step approach or "model"

VARIATIONS AND NOTES

- ☑ Select the topic for each group or for the group as a whole.

- ☑ Have a topic prepared from a previous training course in order to highlight the process of the exercise. Pick something simple such as making a cup of tea.

- ☑ Once each group has drawn the step by step model, ask delegates to spend a few moments to suggest improvements or time saving measures from the model. This is particularly important if the model is of work or skill related activities from the training course.

SWOT Chart

APPLICATION

A simple and valuable exercise for most skills or business training. Can be used to focus on one single set of skills and for an organisation or group of individuals.

PROCEDURE

- ☑ Draw the SWOT chart on a flip chart page, listing in one column Strengths and the other column Weaknesses.

- ☑ A SWOT analysis is a method used by specialists and business planners to gain a strategic perspective on an issue or situation.

- ☑ Complete the chart for the delegates workplace standards and approach.

- ☑ Distribute flip chart paper and pens.

- ☑ Where they have good practices and skills, list these under Strengths. In areas where hazards and risks exist, or you feel there is room for improvement, list these under Weaknesses. The Opportunities section is self-explanatory; it should list ideas which are not being fully developed and utilised. Threats constitute areas of concern and potential problems.

- ☑ Ask delegates to list their own perception of strengths, weaknesses, opportunities and threats with regard to themselves/a skill/their organisation.

- ☑ Allow 10 minutes.

- ☑ Next form into small groups and ask them to summarise their lists collectively on a flip chart page.

- ☑ Allow 10 minutes.

- ☑ Review and discuss charts one at a time.

RELATED FLIP CHARTS

Driving Forces, Flowcharting, Change Planner.

SWOT Chart

▶ List Strengths and Weaknesses (or areas to improve), Opportunities and Threats (or areas of potential hazard)

Strengths	Weaknesses
Opportunities	**Threats**

FLIP 45

VARIATIONS AND NOTES

- ☑ Give each group a focus for the SWOT Chart, for example, their own personal skills, the company or organisation's standing, marketing analysis or product review.

- ☑ After each group has displayed its chart, highlight that sometimes the same things which could be Opportunities could also be Threats simultaneously. Strengths and Weaknesses are very often the same elements at different ends of the scale. Discuss any similarity and any differences between the groups' analyses.

Team Talents

APPLICATION

A good exercise to either highlight or review skills within a team, department, or group of people.

PROCEDURE

- ☑ Draw the following text (and illustrations) on a flip chart page, explaining that this exercise will allow you to get to know your team members better than you do now and also allow you to share with others and see how others judge your skills and attributes.

- ☑ Form delegates into small groups, or run as a main group discussion.

- ☑ Use different coloured pens for different people.

- ☑ Allow 10 - 15 minutes.

RELATED FLIP CHARTS

Six Point Profile, If I Were ….

VARIATIONS AND NOTES

- ☑ Allow time for people to update their exercises as they get to know and work with their colleagues.

Team Talents

▶ Write the names of the team at random on a flip chart page

▶ Through discussion attribute qualities to each person and write against their name

Alice - serious good with numbers

Gary - sense of humour

Bob - Happy, Bold

Francis - leadership skills

Team Solutions

APPLICATION

A good and highly practical way of focusing on how best to implement new ideas and improvements.

PROCEDURE

- ☑ Draw the suggested text and illustration on a flip chart, varying the time limit according to the nature of your obstacle.

- ☑ Form delegates into syndicates of 3 - 7 people.

- ☑ Explain that each group should identify a stumbling block, obstacle or solution they might, or do, face. Write these on a flip chart page.

- ☑ Allow 10 minutes or longer for syndicates to generate as many ideas as possible.

- ☑ Re-convene the main group in a circle around the flip chart.

- ☑ Post up one page at a time and review ideas and suggestions.

RELATED FLIP CHARTS

Brainstorming, Mind Map, Problem-solving, Graffiti.

VARIATIONS AND NOTES

- ☑ Give delegates or syndicates problems to solve that you have collected earlier, transferring items from the Parking Lot or objectives that you did not intend to cover fully in the training course.

- ☑ Ask delegates to spend 5 minutes working individually listing their own ideas for solutions to a problem or obstacle, before working together in a syndicate or team. This will highlight that two heads really are often better than one in this kind of situation.

Team Solutions

▶ Identify an obstacle to implementing today's ideas

▶ Take 10 minutes to brainstorm ways to overcome it

FLIP 47

Taking Sides

APPLICATION

A good exercise to generate discussion and group interaction.

PROCEDURE

- ☑ Draw the diagram and instructions on a flip chart, writing a controversial statement or point of view in the box.

- ☑ Ask delegates to think about this statement and move to either the front (for/agree) or back of the room (against/disagree).

- ☑ Each group (those at the front and those at the back) have 10 minutes to discuss their views and prepare the arguments for and against.

- ☑ Chair a short debate between the two sides with delegates contributing freely from each group.

- ☑ After time is up, or agreement has been reached, discuss issues arising and the approach taken by each side.

RELATED FLIP CHARTS

Hopes and Concerns.

VARIATIONS AND NOTES

- ☑ By shortening the discussion time you can run this exercise several times with different controversial statements or viewpoints.

- ☑ Be particularly alert for people who change their minds and try to disguise why they had their change of view, or people who have one opinion which is different from their own day to day behaviour. For example, a view that 'All smoking should be made illegal' may actually be supported by somebody who smokes.

Taking Sides

▶ Consider the point below carefully

▶ Decide if you are FOR or AGAINST and move to the FRONT or BACK of the room

▶ Take 10 minutes to prepare your arguments

▶ Debate for 10 minutes or until agreement is reached

OPINION

FLIP 48

Top Ten Ideas

APPLICATION

An easy and effective way to summarise the training content from a course session.

This is a particularly useful exercise to run at the end of a training session or a training day on a multiple day course. It reviews the key learning points from any event in a non-competitive and a very practical manner. It combines both quiet individual review together with team discussion.

PROCEDURE

- ☑ Draw the instructions on a flip chart page.

- ☑ Ask delegates to spend 3 to 4 minutes quietly reviewing and reading through their notes for the last session of the training course as a whole.

- ☑ Form delegates into small teams, with 3 - 5 in each.

- ☑ Ask each team to determine 10 ideas or tips from the session, discuss the relative importance of each and then list on a flip chart page in order of importance.

- ☑ Allow 10 - 15 minutes.

- ☑ Post pages around the room.

- ☑ Discuss differences or similarities between sheets.

RELATED FLIP CHARTS

Quick Quiz, Keys to Success, Seven Question Summary.

VARIATIONS AND NOTES

- ☑ Instead of 10 ideas, 3 or 5 are enough if a shorter training session is required.

- ☑ Discuss whether the things they have learned or the things they have found to be most important from the course were things they already knew but had forgotten.

Top Ten Ideas

▶ Review everything that has been covered today

▶ List the 10 most important points on flip chart page in order of importance

FLIP 49

Training Standards

APPLICATION

A good exercise to run at the start of any course or event.

Different people will have different expectations. Some may have attended many training courses in the past and they will therefore be very familiar with what to expect and how to contribute; others less so. It is also important to recognise that different organisations may have different expectations or standards they require from the trainer or presenter. This is a way of beginning to measure and define the standards and expectations.

PROCEDURE

- ☑ Draw text onto a flip chart and ask delegates to copy into their notes.

- ☑ Before setting the exercise, run through some examples of the kind of headings or thoughts the delegates might want to consider. For example, how would they like the trainer or presenter to act and facilitate the course? What facilities are important to them in a training environment? What is their preference for breaks? What level of activities, interaction and discussion would they prefer? How would someone in their position as a delegate or attendee need to behave or act to get the very best from the training course?

- ☑ Explain that this exercise is designed to establish "best practice" for both trainer and delegates; things that will ensure learning objectives are achieved in an enjoyable fashion.

- ☑ Ask delegates to work in small groups and list five points or ideas in each column.

- ☑ Allow 10 - 15 minutes.

- ☑ Post around the room and review.

RELATED FLIP CHARTS

Hopes and Concerns.

Training Standards

▶ Discuss and list how everyone can get the best from this training course

VARIATIONS AND NOTES

- ☑ Instead of just suggesting headings, actually write them down and ask delegates to consider each one in turn.

- ☑ As a variation, ask delegates to consider other training courses and discuss what they liked or did not like about those particular events.

APPENDIX

QUOTATIONS

REBUSES

SOLUTIONS TO PUZZLE PHRASES

APPENDIX

Quotations

DISPLAY AN INTERESTING OR THOUGHT PROVOKING QUOTATION ON A FLIP CHART PAGE AS DELEGATES ENTER THE TRAINING ROOM?

Whatever you can do, or dream you can ... begin it . For Boldness has Genius, Power and Magic in it. Begin it NOW!!

Goethe

He worked by day
And toiled by night
He gave up play
And some delight.
Dry books he read
New things to learn,
And forged ahead
Success to earn.
He plodded on
With faith and pluck,
And when he won
They called it luck.

Anon

A generous man will prosper; he who refreshes others will himself be refreshed.

Proverbs 11:25

Folks who never do any more than they get paid for, never get paid for any more than they do.

Elbert Hubbard

People who say something can't be done are usually interrupted by those doing it!

Anon

People who would never think of committing suicide or ending their lives would think nothing of dribbling their lives away in useless minutes and hours every day.

Thomas Carlyle

Five percent of the people think, ten percent of the people think they think; and the other eighty-five percent would rather die than think.

Anon

Opportunity is often missed because we are broadcasting when we should be tuning in.

Anon

If one advances confidently in the direction of his own dreams and endeavours to live the life which he has imagined, he will meet with a success unexpected in common hours.

Henry David Thoreau

Life is a battle from the beginning to the end. One of the biggest battles you will ever have will be with yourself.

Dr Norman Vincent Peale

Not everything that is faced can be changed, but nothing can be changed until it is faced.

James Baldwin

Most people plan their vacations better than they plan their lives.

Mary Kay Ash

Self doubt is nothing but a cover-up of innate strengths. Confidence is nothing but a cover-up of our weaknesses. True confidence comes from our ability to uncover and accept our weaknesses and to discover and use our strengths.

Gerhard Gschwandtner

Winners never quit. Quitters never win.

Vince Lombardi

Don't forget until too late that the business of life is not business, but living.

B. C. Forbes

It takes less effort to keep an old customer satisfied than to get a new customer interested.

Anon

Life has been given to us, therefore it doesn't owe us anything.

Gerhard Gschwandtner

If you can't write your idea on the back of a business card, you don't have a clear idea.

Anon

A word is not a crystal, transparent and unchanged; it is the skin of a living thought that may vary greatly in colour and content according to the circumstances in which it is used.

Oliver Wendell Holmes

Lack of activity destroys the good condition of every human being, while movement and methodical physical exercise save and preserve it.

Plato

A mistake at least proves somebody stopped talking long enough to do something.

Anon

Talking is like playing the harp. There is as much in laying the hand on the strings to stop their vibrations as in twanging them to bring out their music.

Oliver Wendell Holmes

Problems are nothing but wake-up calls for creativity.

Anon

The tougher you are on yourself, the easier life will be on you.

Zig Ziglar

People who are lost in their lives tend to follow people who are lost in their theories.

Roger Gentis

The only place where success comes before work is in the dictionary.

Anon

You can make more friends in two months by becoming really interested in other people than you can in two years by trying to get other people interested in you.

Dale Carnegie

We act as though comfort and luxury were the chief requirements of life, when all that we need to make us really happy is something to be enthusiastic about.

Anon

Adversity is the diamond dust heaven polishes its jewels with!

Robert Leighton

Don't cut your life into years, weeks or days, but cut your days into lives. Then celebrate each moment as one full life.

Gerhard Gschwandtner

We become what we think about. If we don't think, we become nothing.

Earl Nightingale

You must make your mark on this earth, and, if you have never done so, it is simply because you neglected to use the powers you have, or have neglected to develop them.

John Henry Patterson

When your mind is tired, exercise your body, when your body is tired, exercise your mind.

Anon

Nothing in the world can take the place of persistence.

Talent will not: nothing is more common than unsuccessful men with talent.

Genius will not: unrewarded genius is almost a proverb.

Education will not: the world is full of educated derelicts.

Persistence and determination alone are omnipotent.

The slogan "press on" has solved and always will solve the problems of human race.

President Calvin Coolidge

The best time to complete your daily plan is the night before. That way you'll wake up motivated and you won't be floundering around for half a day just defining what you want to accomplish.

Tom Hopkins

Do a disagreeable job today instead of tomorrow. You will save 24 hours of dreading to do it, while having 24 hours to savour the feeling that the job is behind you.

Anon

Worry is misuse of the imagination.

Mary Crowley

If you would hit the mark, you must aim a little above it: Every arrow that flies feels the attraction of earth.

Longfellow

The three great essentials to achieve anything worthwhile are first, hard work; second, stick-to-itiveness; third, common sense.

Thomas A. Edison

Quality IS productivity.

Federal Express management manual

Try not to become a man of success but rather try to become a man of value.

Einstein

Imagination is more important than knowledge.

Einstein

Courage is the first of human qualities because it is the quality which guarantees all the others.

Winston Churchill

If we open a quarrel between the past and the present, we shall find that we have lost the future.

Winston Churchill

The empires of the future are the empires of the mind.

Winston Churchill

For a man to achieve all that is demanded of him he must regard himself as greater than he is.

Goethe

Our life is what our thoughts make it.

Marcus Aurelius

The desire of gold is not for gold. It is for the means of freedom and benefit.

Emerson

Flip Chart Games for Trainers

When I was young I thought that money was the most important thing in life; now that I am old I know that it is.

Oscar Wilde

The aim of education should be to teach us rather how to think, than what to think; rather to improve our minds, so as to enable us to think for ourselves, than to load the memory with the thoughts of other men.

James BeattieDo or don't do, there is no try.

Anon

It is a descending stream of pure activity which is the dynamic force of the universe.

Kabbalah

Enthusiasm is the leaping-lightning little understood by the horse-power of the understanding.

Emerson

Whether you believe you can, or whether you believe you can't - you're right!

Henry T. Ford

Learning is a kind of natural food for the mind.

Cicero

You cannot teach a man anything; you can only help him to find it within himself.

Galileo

Each day is the scholar of yesterday.

Publilius Syrus

Reading maketh a full man; confidence a ready man; and writing an exact man.

Bacon

Crafty men condemn studies, simple men admire them, and wise men use them.

Bacon

Some men grow mad by studying much to know, but who grows mad by studying good to grow?

Franklin

Seeing much, suffering much, and studying much, are the three pillars of learning.

Disraeli

The best education in the world is that got by struggling to get a living.

Wendell Phillips

There are three schoolmasters for everybody that will employ them ... the senses, intelligent companions, and books.

Beecher

To know how to suggest is the great art of teaching.

Henri Frederic Amiel

Reading and writing, arithmetic and grammar do not constitute education, any more than a knife, fork and spoon constitute a dinner.

Lubbock

Education is what survives when what has been learnt has been forgotten.

F. Skinner

How much you know is less important than how fast you are learning.

Anon

Only the educated are free.

Epictetus

Education is leading human souls to what is best, and making what is best out of them; and these two objects are always attainable together, and by the same means; the training which makes men happiest in themselves also makes them most serviceable to others.

John Ruskin

Knowledge increases in proportion to its use, that is, the more we teach the more we learn.

P. Blavatsky

Learning is weightless ... treasure you always carry easily.

Chinese Proverb

What we have to learn to do, we learn by doing.

Aristotle

Study what thou art
Whereof thou art a part
What thou knowest of this art
This is really what thou art.
All that is without thee also is within.

Solomon Trismosin

To waken interest and kindle enthusiasm is the sure way to teach easily and successfully.

Tryon Edwards

The most valuable result of all education is the ability to make yourself do the thing you have to do, when it ought to be done, whether you like it or not.

Thomas Huxley

Never regard study as a duty but as an enviable opportunity to learn to know the liberating influence of beauty in the realm of the spirit for your own personal joy and to the profit of the community to which your later works belong.

Einstein

And still they gazed, and still the wonder grew, That one small head should carry all it knew.

Goldsmith

He might have been a very clever man by nature, but he had laid so many books on his head that his brain could not move.

Robert Hall

One impulse from a vernal wood
May teach you more of man,
Of moral evil and of good,
Than all the sages can.

Wordsworth

The important thing is not to stop questioning.

Einstein

Teachers open the door ... you enter by yourself.

Chinese Proverb

The process of scientific discovery is, in effect, a continual flight from wonder.

Einstein

Flip Chart Games for Trainers

Rebuses

…… help build a humour-laden atmosphere………………..

> Use to introduce any session on creativity or problem-solving
>
> Use as a "just for fun" or a "change of pace" activity
>
> Draw on the flip chart and suggest that each block represents a well-known phrase or saying.

REBUS 1

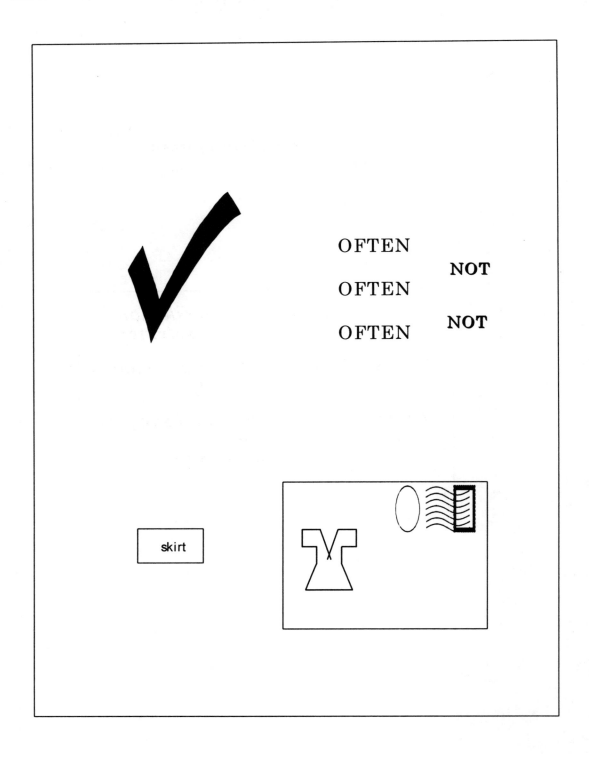

REBUS 2

REBUS 3

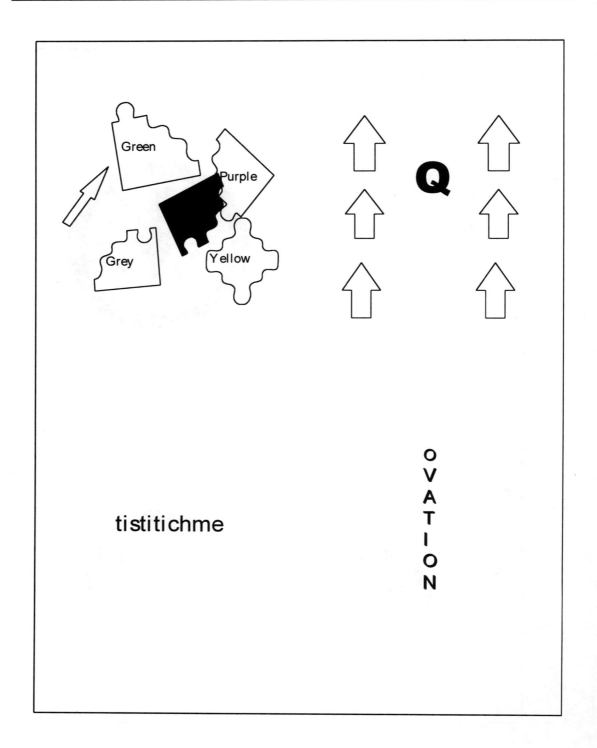

REBUS 4

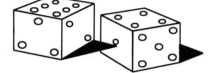   L NCH
              L NCH

VA DERS   NO NO
                CORRECT

Rebus 5

Rebus 6

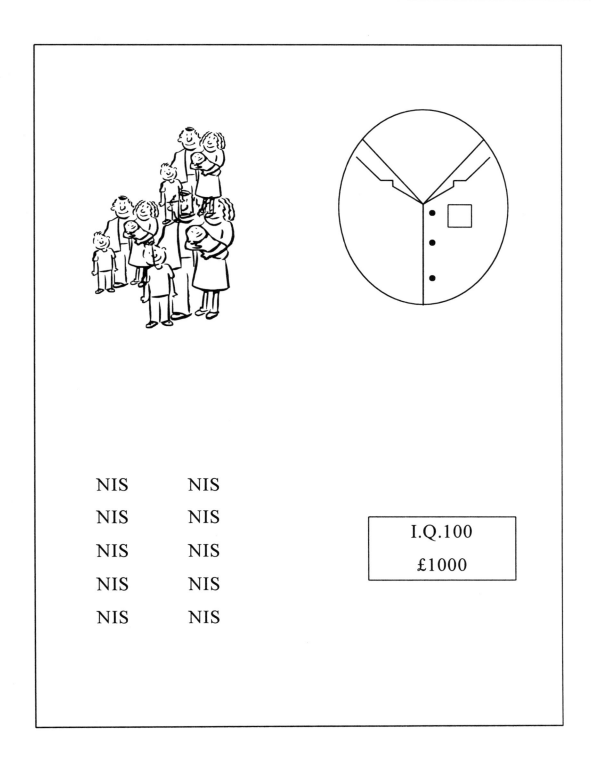

REBUS 7

one decibel

HELL

RTUVVWXZ

POD
POD
POD

REBUS 8

Solutions to Puzzle Phrases

Rebus 1
- Just a tick
- More often than not
- Mini skirt
- Address

Rebus 2
- Banana split
- Spokesman
- Money talks
- Time flies

Rebus 3
- Green Peace
- Queue up
- Stitch in time
- Standing ovation

Rebus 4
- Paradise
- Take you out to lunch
- Space Invaders
- Right under your nose

Rebus 5
- Mixed doubles
- Last but not least
- Weather cock
- Jail birds

Rebus 6
- Happy families
- Jacket Potato
- Tennis
- More money than sense

Rebus 7
- A quiet period
- Hello
- Tripod
- Nosy

Rebus 8
- Time and time again
- Space suit
- Originate
- Slip knot

Action Learning in Practice

Third Edition

Edited by Mike Pedler

Since it first appeared in 1983, *Action Learning in Practice* has established itself, alongside the writings of Professor Reg Revans, as the standard work on the subject. It is unique in covering the theory, practice and implementation of Action Learning in one volume.

This third edition, with no fewer than eleven new chapters, reflects the continued growth in Action Learning and related management development methods. It contains contributions from most of the leading exponents of AL, including Reg Revans himself.

In Part I a number of experienced practitioners present their views on the nature of Action Learning. Part II comprises eight case studies drawn from a wide variety of organizations around the world. Part III looks at some of the key aspects of designing and running AL programmes, and a newly created Part IV describes ways of evaluating the AL approach. Supporting material includes a detailed review of the AL literature compiled by Professor Alan Mumford.

This enlarged and updated edition is sure of a warm welcome from all managers and professionals concerned with improving the effectiveness of their people and organizations.

Gower

Developing Managers Through Project-Based Learning

Bryan Smith and Bob Dodds

Every educator knows that the most effective way to learn is by 'doing' - and nowhere is that truth more clearly seen than in management development. This wide-ranging book explains what is involved in planning and running project-based management development programmes and demonstrates the benefits for both the individuals and the organizations concerned.

Drawing on the unrivalled experience of PA-Sundridge Park Management Centre in this field, the authors:

- show how to set up the necessary frameworks
- describe programmes for different levels of management, including 'top teams'
- examine the role of the sponsor
- point out the potential pitfalls and indicate how to avoid them
- look at the influence of national culture.

With summaries and checklists, and case studies focusing on ICI, Allied Domecq, Volvo, Gestetner, Lloyds Bank Insurance Services, The Inland Revenue, London Underground and others, the emphasis throughout is very much on the practical.

For anyone concerned with improving managerial performance, this is a book that will repay careful study.

Gower

The Excellent Trainer

Putting NLP to Work

Di Kamp

Most trainers are familiar with the principles of Neuro-Linguistic Programming. What Di Kamp does in her latest book is to show how NLP techniques can be directly applied to the business of training.

Kamp looks first at the fast-changing organizational world in which trainers now operate, then at the role of the trainer and the skills and qualities required. She goes on to deal with the actual training process and provides systematic guidance on using NLP in preparation, delivery and follow-up. Finally she explores the need for continuous improvement, offering not only ideas and explanation but also instruments and activities designed to enhance both personal and professional development.

If you are involved in training, you'll find this book a powerful tool both for developing yourself and for enriching the learning opportunities you create for others.

Gower

Games for Trainers

3 Volume Set

Andy Kirby

Most trainers use games. And trainers who use games collect new games. Andy Kirby's three-volume compendium contain 75 games in each volume. They range from icebreakers and energizers to substantial exercises in communication. Each game is presented in a standard format which includes summary, statement of objectives, list of materials required, recommended timings and step-by-step instructions for running the event. Photocopiable masters are provided for any materials needed by participants.

All the games are indexed by objectives, and Volume 1 contains an introduction analysing the different kinds of game, setting out the benefits they offer and explaining how to use games to the maximum advantage. It is a programmed text designed to help trainers to develop their own games. Volume 3 reflects current trends in training; in particular the increased attention being paid to stress management and assertiveness. Volumes 2 and 3 contain an integrated index covering all three volumes.

Gower

Handbook of Management Games and Simulations

Sixth Edition

Edited by Chris Elgood

What kinds of management games are there? How do they compare with other methods of learning? Where can I find the most suitable games for the training objectives I have in mind?

Handbook of Management Games and Simulations provides detailed answers to these questions and many others.

Part 1 of the *Handbook* examines the characteristics and applications of the different types of game. It explains how they promote learning and the circumstances for which they are best suited.

Part 2 comprises a detailed directory of some 300 games and simulations. Each one is described in terms of its target group, subject area, nature and purpose, and the means by which the outcome is established and made known. The entries also contain administrative data including the number of players, the number of teams and the time required. Several indexes enable readers to locate precisely those games that would be relevant for their own needs.

This sixth edition has been revised to reflect recent developments. And of course the directory has been completely updated. Chris Elgood's *Handbook* will continue to be indispensable for anyone concerned with management development.

Gower